Hymns & Songs

A Supplement to
The Methodist Hymn Book

LONDON

Methodist Publishing House

1969

PRINTED IN GREAT BRITAIN BY
NOVELLO AND COMPANY LIMITED
BOROUGH GREEN · KENT

PREFACE

Hymns and Songs owes its publication to a decision of the Methodist Conference in 1965, but it is offered to all Christians.

Many of the hymns were written in the present century and a considerable proportion in this decade, and are in an idiom and style which answer the demand for more contemporary expressions and themes. Others, although more traditional, preserve that directness of statement which congregations now welcome. The book is published at a time when lively discussions on hymnody are going on within the churches, and a great many items of an experimental nature are being written for Christians to sing. Many of these would not claim to be of more than passing interest; others are suitable only for use by solo voices or specialised groups. These do not seem likely to find a permanent place in congregational worship as normally understood at present. This does not imply an adverse judgement about their quality or value, but it would question their suitability for a collection intended to serve for some years. At the same time there are sets of words which do not conform to the more usual patterns but which Christians who are responsive to new creative impulses ought to receive with sympathy. For this reason a section entitled *Songs* has been included. This contains a representative selection of words and music which can be used in worship, but which are not immediately identifiable as hymns.

Hymns and Songs is also devised as a Supplement to *The Methodist Hymn Book*, which was published in 1933. To a certain extent this explains the character of the selection which has been made. Many hymns which might have been included would not have added significantly to what is already in *The Methodist Hymn Book*. The Supplement is not intended as a substitute for the latter, which remains unique in Christendom because of the large number of hymns by John and Charles Wesley, which provide the classic expression of the message and spirit of Methodism.

Hymns and Songs makes available many tunes not in the larger book. Some are published here for the first time. Taken as a whole they are catholic in style and origin. In the interests of congregational singing they are generally set out in fairly low keys. The compilers are aware that this is a matter for debate, but on the whole they are persuaded that the claims of the majority of singers should be given precedence. To facilitate the learning of many of the new or more ambitious hymns their tunes are presented with the melody on a separate stave. For the same reason, and in keeping with recent trends, a Words and Melody edition has been provided for those who do not require a copy with full harmony.

A small section, *Canticles and Psalms*, has been added to introduce a few examples of a method of setting out and singing these ancient hymns which can help to make them more effectively congregational. A selection of *Supplementary Tunes* completes the book. Some of these may be already well known: the others, it is hoped, will be explored as stimulating alternatives.

Because the Supplement is not intended as a complete hymn-book the items have been printed in alphabetical order of first lines, but an index suggesting suitable occasions for many of the hymns has been included.

Since John Wesley wrote his celebrated Preface to the Hymn Book of 1779, the fashions of 'Poetry' have changed and the word 'Piety' has been debased; but we hope as fervently as he that words and music, in whatever forms, may inspire devotion to Our Lord among Methodists and throughout the whole Church of Christ, and proclaim, in our world, that Gospel which is old, yet ever new.

Easter, 1969

ACKNOWLEDGEMENTS

The Editors desire to express their obligation to many authors, composers, and owners or holders of copyright for permission to use hymns and tunes, according to the lists below. Every effort has been made to trace all copyright-owners; but if, through inadvertence, any surviving rights have been overlooked, the necessary correction will gladly be made in subsequent editions.

HYMNS

Author or Translator	Owner or Controller of Copyright	No. of Hymn
AINGER, G.		76, 99
Alington, C. A.	Props. of Hymns Ancient & Modern	29
Andrew, Father	A. R. Mowbray & Co, Ltd	53
Appleford, P.	J. Weinberger Ltd. From *Thirty 20th-Century Hymn Tunes*	86
Arlott, J.		26
BAYLY, A. F.		44, 56, 59
Bethel, R. A.	Mrs Bethel	54
Bridges, R.	Oxford University Press	
	From *The Yattendon Hymnal*	65
Briggs, G. W.	From *Hymns of the Faith*	9, 13, 25
CAIRD, G. B.		49
Carter, S.	Copyright 1961 Sydney Carter. Assigned 1968 to Galliard Ltd. Copyright 1969 from *Sydney Carter in the Present Tense* published by Galliard Ltd.	77
„	Copyright 1963 Sydney Carter. Assigned 1968 to Galliard Ltd. Copyright 1969 from *Sydney Carter in the Present Tense* published by Galliard Ltd.	82
„	Copyright 1964 Sydney Carter. Assigned 1968 to Galliard Ltd. Copyright 1969 from *Sydney Carter in the Present Tense* published by Galliard Ltd.	91
„	Copyright 1965 Sydney Carter. Assigned 1968 to Galliard Ltd. Copyright 1969 from *Sydney Carter in the Present Tense* published by Galliard Ltd.	97
Chisholm, Miss E.		88, 103
„ „ „	Props. Hymns Ancient & Modern	90
DARBYSHIRE, J. R.	Mr C. R. Darbyshire	39
EVANGELICAL SISTERS OF MARY (DARMSTADT)		81
FOSDICK, H. E.		24
Fraser, I.		87
GEYER, J. B.		72, 78
Green, F. Pratt	Oxford University Press	8, 20, 51, 66, 70, 74, 85, 98
Gelineau, J.	The Grail Ltd.	101, 102

Composer or Arranger	Owner or Controller of Copyright	No. of Hymn
Routley, E.	Galliard Ltd. From *New Songs for the Church* published by Galliard Ltd, in association with the Scottish Churches Council . . .	100
SCHWEIZER, R. . . .	Haenssler-Verlag, Stuttgart-Hohenheim . .	43(*ii*)
Sheldon, R.		85
Slater, G.	Oxford University Press	
	From *Songs of Praise for Boys and Girls* .	58
Somervell, A. . . .	The Abbot of Downside	36
Stanford, C. V. . . .	Stainer & Bell Ltd	72
Stewart, M.		95
Sykes, J. A.	Miss C. M. Sykes	S.T.25
TAYLOR, C. V. . . .	Oxford University Press	
	From *The BBC Hymn Book*	42
Thiman, Eric H. . .		S.T.20
WATSON, S.		39, 43(*i*)
Webber, L.		15
Westbrook, F. B. . .	Oxford University Press	21, 23, 53, 90, S.T.13, S.T.21
Williamson, M. . . .	J. Weinberger Ltd	30
Wilson, J.	Oxford University Press	2, 46, 48, 56, 64(*ii*), 68
Wood, C.	Oxford University Press	11
ZIMMERMANN, H. W. .	Bärenreiter & Co	80

HARMONISATION

CLEALL, C.		84
JONES, I. H.		88, 95, 97
LEY, H. G.	Oxford University Press	29
McKIE, W.		S.T.5
VAUGHAN WILLIAMS, R.	Oxford University Press	8, 19, 26, S.T.15
WESTBROOK, F. B. . .	Oxford University Press	38, 75, 83, 93
WOOD, C.	Faith Press Ltd	63(*ii*)
YOUNG, C. R. . . .	Abingdon Press	94

CONTENTS

EXPLANATION

† added to an Author's name denotes a small alteration of his original text.

‡ denotes a more considerable alteration.

Amen is printed only when a musical setting requires it.

'M.H.B.' refers to *The Methodist Hymn Book* (1933).

'S.T.' refers to the *Supplementary Tunes* in this book.

1

J. Stainer (1840–1901)

(It may be desirable to sing this tune a semitone lower.)

For the Love of Jesus

ALL for Jesus—all for Jesus,
This our song shall ever be:
For we have no hope, nor Saviour,
If we have not hope in thee.

2 All for Jesus—thou wilt give us
Strength to serve thee, hour by hour;
None can move us from thy presence,
While we trust thy love and power.

3 All for Jesus—thou hast loved us;
All for Jesus—thou hast died;
All for Jesus—thou art with us;
All for Jesus Crucified.

4 All for Jesus—all for Jesus—
This the Church's song must be;
Till, at last, her sons are gathered
One in love and one in thee.

W. J. Sparrow-Simpson (1859–1952)

2

LALEHAM 10 10 10.4.   JOHN WILSON (1905–   )
Unison

1 All praise to thee, for thou, O King div - ine,

Didst— yield the glo - ry that of right was thine,

That in our dark-ened hearts thy grace might shine:

Al – le – lu – ia, Al-le-lu – – ia!

Philippians 2. 5-11

ALL praise to thee, for thou, O King divine,
Didst yield the glory that of right was thine,
That in our darkened hearts thy grace might shine:
Alleluia!

2 Thou cam'st to us in lowliness of thought;
By thee the outcast and the poor were sought,
And by thy death was God's salvation wrought:
Alleluia!

3 Let this mind be in us which was in thee,
Who wast a servant that we might be free,
Humbling thyself to death on Calvary:
Alleluia!

4 Wherefore, by God's eternal purpose, thou
Art high exalted o'er all creatures now,
And given the name to which all knees shall bow:
Alleluia!

5 Let every tongue confess with one accord
In heav'n and earth that Jesus Christ is Lord;
And God the Father be by all adored:
Alleluia!

F. Bland Tucker (1895-   )

See overleaf for optional harmony version of Verses 2 and 3.

2 *(continued)*

OPTIONAL HARMONY VERSION FOR VERSES 2 & 3

2 Thou cam'st to us in low - li - ness of thought;
3 Let this mind be in us which was in thee,
By— thee the out - cast and the poor were sought,
Who— wast a ser - vant that we might be free,
And by thy death was God's sal - va - tion wrought:
Humb - ling thy - self to death on Cal - va - ry:
(Small notes Organ only)
Al - le - lu - ia, Al - le - lu - - ia!
Al - le - lu - ia, Al - le - lu - - ia!
Al - le - lu - ia, Al - le - lu - - ia!

(In Verse 5 the Tenor part of the 'Alleluias' may be sung as a Descant by Sopranos and Tenors.)

Turn back for Verse 4.

Music: © *Oxford University Press.* *Words:* © *The Church Hymnal Corporation.*

3

BIRABUS 87.87.
Unison

PETER CUTTS (1937–   )

1 All who love and serve your ci - ty, all who bear its daily stress,

all who cry for peace and jus-tice, all who curse and all who bless,

'The Lord is there'

ALL who love and serve your city,
all who bear its daily stress,
all who cry for peace and justice,
all who curse and all who bless,

2 in your day of loss and sorrow,
in your day of helpless strife,
honour, peace and love retreating,
seek the Lord, who is your life.

3 In your day of wealth and plenty,
wasted work and wasted play,
call to mind the word of Jesus,
'Work ye yet while it is day'.

4 For all days are days of judgment,
and the Lord is waiting still,
drawing near to men who spurn him,
offering peace from Calvary's hill.

5 Risen Lord! shall yet the city
be the city of despair?
Come today, our Judge, our Glory;
be its name, 'The Lord is there!'

Erik Routley (1917–   )

3 (continued)

SECOND TUNE

CITIZENS 87.87.
Unison

WILLIAM LLEWELLYN (1925–   )

1 All who love and serve your ci - ty, all who bear its dai - ly stress, all who cry for peace and jus - tice, all who curse and all who bless, be its name, 'The Lord is there!'

The final Descant-note C may also be sung by the Congregation.

Music: © Rydal School Endowment Fund. Words: © Galliard Ltd.

'The Lord is there'

ALL who love and serve your city,
all who bear its daily stress,
all who cry for peace and justice,
all who curse and all who bless,

2 in your day of loss and sorrow,
in your day of helpless strife,
honour, peace and love retreating,
seek the Lord, who is your life.

3 In your day of wealth and plenty,
wasted work and wasted play,
call to mind the word of Jesus,
'Work ye yet while it is day'.

4 For all days are days of judgment,
and the Lord is waiting still,
drawing near to men who spurn him,
offering peace from Calvary's hill.

5 Risen Lord! shall yet the city
be the city of despair?
Come today, our Judge, our Glory;
be its name, 'The Lord is there!'

Erik Routley (1917-   )

4

LANSDOWNE L.M.

E. Norman Greenwood (1902–62)

Unison

1 All ye that seek the Lord who died, Your God for sin-ners cru-ci-fied, Now, now let all your grief be o'er! Be - lieve, and ye shall weep no more.

Alternative Tune, ST BARTHOLOMEW: *see* NO 47, *or* M.H.B.895
Music: © Mrs. Greenwood.

'He is Risen'

ALL ye that seek the Lord who died,
Your God for sinners crucified,
Now, now let all your grief be o'er!
Believe, and ye shall weep no more.

2 The Lord of life is risen indeed,
To death delivered in your stead;
His rise proclaims your sins forgiven,
And shows the living way to heaven.

3 Haste then, ye souls that first believe,
Who dare the gospel word receive,
Your faith with joyful hearts confess,
Be bold, be Jesus' witnesses.

4 Go tell the followers of your Lord
Their Jesus is to life restored;
He lives, that they his life may find;
He lives to quicken all mankind.

Charles Wesley (1707-88)

5

RUTH C.M. C. HINDMARSH (1892–)

1 Be-hold the a-ma-zing gift of love The Fa-ther hath be-stowed

On us, the sin-ful sons of men, To call us sons of God!

Alternative Tune, ABRIDGE, M.H.B. 519

1 *John* 3. 1-4

Behold the amazing gift of love
 The Father hath bestowed
On us, the sinful sons of men,
 To call us sons of God!

2 Concealed as yet this honour lies,
 By this dark world unknown,
A world that knew not when he came,
 Ev'n God's eternal Son.

3 High is the rank we now possess;
 But higher we shall rise;
Though what we shall hereafter be
 Is hid from mortal eyes:

4 Our souls, we know, when he appears,
 Shall bear his image bright;
For all his glory, full disclosed,
 Shall open to our sight.

5 A hope so great and so divine
 May trials well endure;
And purge the soul from sense and sin,
 As Christ himself is pure.

Scottish Paraphrases (1781)

6

FIRST TUNE

GREESTONE 66.88.6.

Unison. About ♩=96

IVOR H. JONES (1934–   )

Organ (without Ped.)

Ped.

1 Be-yond —— the mist and doubt Of this un - cer-tain day, / I trust in thine e - ter - nal name, Be yond all / chan - ges still the same, And in that name I pray.

2 Our rest - less in - tel - lect Has all things in its shade, / But still to thee my spi - rit clings, Se rene be - / yond all sha-ken things, And I am not a - fraid.

3 Still in —— hu - mi - li - ty We know thee by thy grace, / For sci - en-ce's re - mo - test probe, Feels but the / frin - ges of thy robe: Love looks up - on thy face.

Music: © Ivor H. Jones. Words: © J. R. Hughes.

Donald Hughes (1911-67)

6 (*continued*)

SECOND TUNE

REQUIEM 66.88.6.
Unison. Rather slowly

WILLIAM LLEWELLYN (1925–)

1 Be-yond the mist and doubt Of this un-cer-tain day,

I trust in thine e-ter-nal name, Be-yond all chan-ges still the

same, And in that name___ I pray.

Music: © *Rydal School Endowment Fund. Words:* © *J. R. Hughes.*

Credo

Beyond the mist and doubt
Of this uncertain day,
I trust in thine eternal name,
Beyond all changes still the same,
And in that name I pray.

2   Our restless intellect
Has all things in its shade,
But still to thee my spirit clings,
Serene beyond all shaken things,
And I am not afraid.

3   Still in humility
We know thee by thy grace,
For science's remotest probe
Feels but the fringes of thy robe:
Love looks upon thy face.

Donald Hughes (1911-67)

7

WESTMINSTER ABBEY 87.87.87.

Moving freely, and not too slowly

Adapted from an anthem
of HENRY PURCELL (c.1659–1695)

Urbs beata Jerusalem

BLESSED City, heavenly Salem,
  Vision dear of peace and love,
Who of living stones art builded
  In the height of heaven above,
And by angel hosts encircled
  As a bride dost earthward move!

2 Christ is made the sure Foundation,
    Christ the Head and Corner-stone,
  Chosen of the Lord, and precious,
    Binding all the Church in one,
  Holy Zion's help for ever,
    And her confidence alone.

3 To this temple, where we call thee,
    Come, O Lord of Hosts, today;
  With thy wonted loving-kindness
    Hear thy servants as they pray;
  And thy fullest benediction
    Shed within its walls alway.

4 Here vouchsafe to all thy servants
    What they ask of thee to gain,
  What they gain from thee for ever
    With the blessèd to retain,
  And hereafter in thy glory
    Evermore with thee to reign.

From the Latin, probably 6th or 7th century
Tr. J. M. Neale‡ (1818-66)

8

CHRISTE SANCTORUM 10 11 11.6.

Melody from *Paris Antiphoner* (1681)
Harmonized by R. Vaughan Williams
(as arranged in *The BBC Hymn Book*, 1951)

Unison

1 Christ is the world's Light, he— and none o-ther; Born in our dark-ness, he be-came our Bro-ther. If we have seen— him, we have seen the Fa - ther: Glo-ry to God on high.

Music and Words: © *Oxford University Press.*

The Uniqueness of Christ

CHRIST is the world's Light, he and none other;
Born in our darkness, he became our Brother.
If we have seen him, we have seen the Father:
    Glory to God on high.

2 Christ is the world's Peace, he and none other;
No man can serve him and despise his brother.
Who else unites us, one in God the Father?
    Glory to God on high.

3 Christ is the world's Life, he and none other;
Sold once for silver, murdered here, our Brother—
He, who redeems us, reigns with God the Father:
    Glory to God on high.

4 Give God the glory, God and none other;
Give God the glory, Spirit, Son and Father;
Give God the glory, God in man my brother:
    Glory to God on high.

F. Pratt Green (1903-   )

9

RINKART 67.67.66.66
(KOMMT SEELEN)
Unison. *Moving freely, and not too slowly.*

Melody and figured bass by
J. S. Bach (1685–1750)

1 {
Christ is— the world's true Light,— Its Cap-tain of— sal –va – tion,
The Day-star shin - ing bright— To ev - ery man— and na - tion;

New life, **new hope** a - wakes,— Where'er— men own— his sway:—

Free – dom her bond– age breaks,— And night— is turned to day.—

*(Small notes
ad lib.)*

In Christ all races meet . . .

CHRIST is the world's true Light,
　　Its Captain of salvation,
The Daystar shining bright
　　To every man and nation;
New life, new hope awakes,
　　Where'er men own his sway:
Freedom her bondage breaks,
　　And night is turned to day.

2 In Christ all races meet,
　　Their ancient feuds forgetting,
The whole round world complete,
　　From sunrise to its setting:
When Christ is throned as Lord,
　　Men shall forsake their fear,
To ploughshare beat the sword,
　　To pruning-hook the spear.

3 One Lord, in one great Name
　　Unite us all who own thee;
Cast out our pride and shame
　　That hinder to enthrone thee;
The world has waited long,
　　Has travailed long in pain;
To heal its ancient wrong,
　　Come, Prince of Peace, and reign.

G. W. Briggs (1875-1959)

10

HANDSWORTH 87.87.D.
Unison

IVOR H. JONES (1934-)

1 Christ, our King before cre-a-tion, Son, who shared the Fa-ther's plan,

Crowned in deep hu-mi-li-a-tion By your friend and partner, man:

Make us hum-ble in be-liev-ing, And, be-liev-ing, bold to pray —

Music: © Ivor H. Jones.

'Lord, for-give our self-de-ceiv-ing, Come and reign in us today!! day!!

Praying for the Kingdom

CHRIST, our King before creation,
  Son, who shared the Father's plan,
Crowned in deep humiliation
  By your friend and partner, man:
Make us humble in believing,
  And, believing, bold to pray—
'Lord, forgive our self-deceiving,
  Come and reign in us today!'

2 Lord of life and Lord of history,
   Giving us, when man despairs,
Faith to wrestle with the mystery
   Of a God who loves and cares:
Make us humble in believing,
   And, believing, bold to pray—
'Lord, by grace beyond conceiving,
   Come and reign in us today!'

3 Word that ends our long debating,
   Word of God that sets us free,
Through your body re-creating
   Man as he is meant to be:
Make us humble in believing,
   And, believing, bold to pray—
'Lord, in us your aim achieving,
   Come and reign in us today!'

                    Ivor H. Jones (1934-   )
                         and compilers

11

CAMBRIDGE 66.65.65.

CHARLES WOOD (1866–1926)

Rather slowly

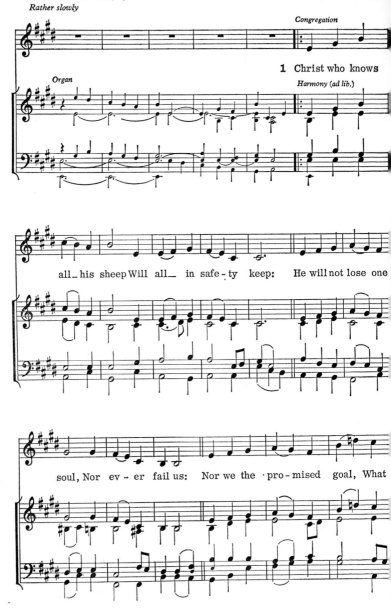

Congregation

1 Christ who knows

Organ

Harmony (ad lib.)

all his sheep Will all in safe-ty keep: He will not lose one

soul, Nor ev-er fail us: Nor we the pro-mised goal, What

e'er as-sail us.

The Life Eternal

CHRIST who knows all his sheep
Will all in safety keep:
He will not lose one soul,
    Nor ever fail us:
Nor we the promised goal,
    Whate'er assail us.

2 We know our God is just;
To him we wholly trust
All that we have and claim,
    And all we hope for:
All's sure and seen to him,
    Which here we grope for.

3 Fear not the World of Light,
Though out of mortal's sight;
There shall we know God more,
    Where all is holy:
There is no grief or care,
    No sin or folly.

4 O Blessèd Company,
Where all in harmony
God's joyous praises sing,
    In love unceasing;
And all obey their King,
    With perfect pleasing!

*Adapted from a poem
by Richard Baxter (1615-91)*

B

COME, MY WAY 77.77.   ALEXANDER BRENT SMITH (1889–1950)

Slow

Unis. 1 Come, my Way, my Truth,— my Life:— Such a
Harm. 2 Come, my Light, my Feast,— my Strength:— Such a

Way, as gives us breath; Such a Truth, as ends all
Light, as shows a feast; Such a Feast, as mends in

strife; Such a Life,——— as kill - eth death.
length; Such a Strength,——— as makes his guest.

Congregation

3 Come, my Joy, my Love,— my Heart: Such a

Organ

(Sop.) Such a
, *Harmony*

(Unison)

Such a

Joy, as none can move; Such a Love, as none can
Joy,_____ Such a Love,_____
Joy, as none can move; Such a Love, as none can

part; Such a Heart,_____ as joys in love.
part; Such a Heart,_____ as joys in love.

(Small notes organ)

The Call

COME, my Way, my Truth, my Life:
    Such a Way, as gives us breath;
    Such a Truth, as ends all strife;
    Such a Life, as killeth death.

2 Come, my Light, my Feast, my Strength:
    Such a Light, as shows a feast;
    Such a Feast, as mends in length;
    Such a Strength, as makes his guest.

3 Come, my Joy, my Love, my Heart:
    Such a Joy, as none can move;
    Such a Love, as none can part;
    Such a Heart, as joys in love.

George Herbert (1593-1633)

The Congregation may prefer to sing from the Melody Version overleaf.

Music: © Miss M. Brent Smith.

12 (continued)

MELODY VERSION

COME, MY WAY

ALEXANDER BRENT SMITH (1889–1950)

Slow

1 Come, my Way, my Truth, my Life:
2 Come, my Light, my Feast, my Strength:
3 Come, my Joy, my Love, my Heart:

Such a Way, as gives us breath;
Such a Light, as shows a feast;
Such a Joy, as none can move;

Such a Truth, as ends all strife;
Such a Feast, as mends in length;
Such a Love, as none can part;

Such a Life, as kill-eth death.
Such a Strength, as makes his guest.
Such a Heart, as joys in love.

George Herbert (1593-1633)

13

WILLIAM H. HARRIS (1883–)

The Feast is Thine ...

COME, risen Lord, and deign to be our guest;
Nay, let us be thy guests: the feast is thine;
Thyself at thine own board make manifest,
In thine own sacrament of bread and wine.

2 We meet, as in that upper room they met;
Thou at the table, blessing, yet dost stand:
'This is my body': so thou givest yet:
Faith still receives the cup as from thy hand.

3 One body we, one body who partake,
One Church united in communion blest;
One name we bear, one bread of life we break,
With all thy saints on earth and saints at rest.

4 One with each other, Lord, for one in thee,
Who art one Saviour and one living Head;
Then open thou our eyes, that we may see;
Be known to us in breaking of the bread.

G. W. Briggs (1875-1959)

BOW BRICKHILL L.M.

S. H. NICHOLSON (1875–1947)

Alternative Tune, NIAGARA, NO. 50

For God's Blessing on our Worship

COMMAND thy blessing from above,
O God, on all assembled here;
Behold us with a Father's love,
While we look up with filial fear.

2 Command thy blessing, Jesus, Lord;
May we thy true disciples be;
Speak to each heart the mighty word,
Say to the weakest, 'Follow me'.

3 Command thy blessing in this hour,
Spirit of Truth, and fill this place
With humbling and exalting power,
With quickening and confirming grace.

4 O thou, our Maker, Saviour, Guide,
One true eternal God confessed:
Whom thou hast joined may none divide,
Nor dare to curse whom thou hast blessed.

5 With thee and these for ever bound,
May all, who here in prayer unite,
With joyful songs thy throne surround,
Rest in thy love, and reign in light.

James Montgomery† (1771–1854)

15

LLOYD WEBBER (1914–)

Penitence

CREATOR of the earth and skies,
To whom all truth and power belong,
Grant us your truth to make us wise;
Grant us your power to make us strong.

2 We have not known you: to the skies
Our monuments of folly soar,
And all our self-wrought miseries
Have made us trust ourselves the more.

3 We have not loved you: far and wide
The wreckage of our hatred spreads,
And evils wrought by human pride
Recoil on unrepentant heads.

4 We long to end this worldwide strife:
How shall we follow in your way?
Speak to mankind your words of life,
Until our darkness turns to day.

Donald Hughes‡ (1911-67)

16

LES COMMANDEMENS 98.98.

Melody from *La Forme des Prieres et Chantz Ecclesiastiques* (Strasbourg, 1545)

1 Fa-ther, we thank thee who hast plan-ted Thy ho-ly name with-in our hearts. Know-ledge and faith and life im-mor-tal Je-sus thy Son to us im-parts.

NOTE—*A regular crotchet beat should be maintained in the first line. The following simpler rhythm may be used if preferred:*

Alternative Tune, RENDEZ À DIEU, M.H.B. 756

The Living Bread

FATHER, we thank thee who hast planted
   Thy holy name within our hearts.
Knowledge and faith and life immortal
   Jesus thy Son to us imparts.

2 Thou, Lord, didst make all for thy pleasure,
   Didst give man food for all his days,
Giving in Christ the bread eternal;
   Thine is the power, be thine the praise.

3 Watch o'er thy Church, O Lord, in mercy,
   Save it from evil, guard it still,
Perfect it in thy love, unite it,
   Cleansed and conformed unto thy will.

4 As grain, once scattered on the hillsides,
   Was in the broken bread made one,
So from all lands thy Church be gathered
   Into thy kingdom by thy Son.

From prayers in the 'Didache', probably 2nd century
Tr. F. Bland Tucker† (1895-   )

Words: © The Church Hymnal Corporation.

17

First Tune

OTTERY ST MARY 87.87.   Henry G. Ley (1887–1962)

DESCANT

Music: © Mrs H. G. Ley.

Later form of a tune by
DR WILLIAM BOYCE (c.1710–1779)
HALTON HOLGATE 87.87. as given in S. S. WESLEY'S *European Psalmist* (1872)

Alternative Tune, CROSS OF JESUS, M.H.B. 318(i)

A Christian's Creed

FIRMLY I believe and truly
    God is Three, and God is One;
And I next acknowledge duly
    Manhood taken by the Son.

2 And I trust and hope most fully
    In that Manhood crucified;
And each thought and deed unruly
    Do to death, as he has died.

3 Simply to his grace and wholly
    Light and life and strength belong,
And I love supremely, solely,
    Him the holy, him the strong.

4 And I hold in veneration,
    For the love of him alone,
Holy Church as his creation,
    And her teachings as his own.

5 Adoration aye be given,
    With and through the angelic host,
To the God of earth and heaven,
    Father, Son, and Holy Ghost.

J. H. Newman (1801-90)
from 'The Dream of Gerontius'

18

Melody, and most of the bass, from
Easy Hymn-Tunes for Catholic Schools (1851)
(based on an 18th-century German melody)

ST BERNARD C.M.

For alternative harmonization, see M.H.B. 408

As we forgive...

'FORGIVE our sins as we forgive'
You taught us, Lord, to pray,
But you alone can grant us grace
To live the words we say.

2 How can your pardon reach and bless
The unforgiving heart
That broods on wrongs and will not let
Old bitterness depart?

3 In blazing light your Cross reveals
The truth we dimly knew,
How small the debts men owe to us,
How great our debt to you!

4 Lord, cleanse the depths within our souls
And bid resentment cease;
Then, reconciled to God and man,
Our lives will spread your peace.

Rosamond E. Herklots (1905-   )

19

English Carol Melody, 15th century
Harmonized by R. Vaughan Williams (1872–1958)

THIS ENDRIS NYGHT   C.M.

The Word made Flesh

A solis ortus cardine

FROM East to West, from shore to shore,
Let earth awake and sing
The holy Child whom Mary bore,
The Christ, the Lord, the King!

2 For lo! the world's Creator wears
The fashion of a slave:
Our human flesh the Godhead bears,
His creature, man, to save.

3 For this how wondrously he wrought!
A maiden, in her place,
Became in ways beyond all thought
The vessel of his grace.

4 He shrank not from the oxen's stall,
Nor scorned the manger-bed;
And he, whose bounty feedeth all,
At Mary's breast was fed.

5 To shepherds poor the Lord most high,
Great Shepherd, was revealed;
While angel-choirs sang joyously
Above the midnight field.

6 All glory be to God above,
And on the earth be peace
To all who long to taste his love,
Till time itself shall cease.

Coelius Sedulius (c. 450)
Tr. J. Ellerton† (1826–93)

20

ILFRACOMBE L.M. with Alleluias

JOHN GARDNER (1917–   )

1 Glor-ious the day when Christ was born
2 Glor-ious the day when Christ a-rose,
3 Glor-ious the days of gos-pel grace
4 Glor-ious the day when Christ ful-fils

Al-le-lu-ia, Al-le-lu-ia, Al-le-lu-ia!

To wear the crown that cae-sars scorn,
The sur-est Friend of all his foes;
When Christ re-stores the fall-en race;
What man re-jects yet fee-bly wills;

Al-le-lu-ia, Al-le-lu-ia, Al-le-lu-ia!

Whose life and death that love re - veal ____
Who for the sake of those he grieves ____
When doubt-ers kneel and wa - verers stand, ____
When that strong Light puts out the sun ____

Al - le-lu - ia, Al - le-lu - ia, Al - le-lu - ia! ____

Which all men need and need to feel. ____
Tran-scends the world he ne - ver leaves. ____
And faith a - chieves what rea - son planned. ____
And all is end - ed, all be - gun. ____

Al - le-lu - ia, Al - le-lu - ia, Al - le-lu - ia!

F. Pratt Green (1903-   )

Music: © John Gardner. Words: © Oxford University Press.

20 (continued)

SECOND TUNE

TRURO L.M.

Altered form of tune (as M.H.B. 272)
(see 2nd version below)

ALTERNATIVE VERSION
(with original form of melody)

TRURO L.M.

Melody from T. WILLIAMS's *Psalmodia Evangelica* (1789)

The Glorious Work of Christ

GLORIOUS the day when Christ was born
To wear the crown that caesars scorn,
Whose life and death that love reveal
Which all men need and need to feel.

2 Glorious the day when Christ arose,
The surest Friend of all his foes;
Who for the sake of those he grieves
Transcends the world he never leaves.

3 Glorious the days of gospel grace
When Christ restores the fallen race;
When doubters kneel and waverers stand,
And faith achieves what reason planned.

4 Glorious the day when Christ fulfils
What man rejects yet feebly wills;
When that strong Light puts out the sun
And all is ended, all begun.

F. Pratt Green (1903-   )

BENIFOLD 8.33.6.D.   FRANCIS WESTBROOK (1903–   )

1 Glo-ry, love, and praise, and hon-our For our food Now be-stowed

Ren-der we the Do — nor. Bounteous God, we now con-fess thee,

God, who thus Bless-est us,   Meet it is to bless thee.

Alternative Tune, BONN, M.H.B. 121

Music: © Oxford University Press.

'Our sacrifice of praise and thanksgiving'

PART 1

GLORY, love, and praise, and honour
For our food
Now bestowed
Render we the Donor.
Bounteous God, we now confess thee,
God, who thus
Blessest us,
Meet it is to bless thee.

2 Knows the ox his master's stable,
And shall we
Not know thee,
Nourished at thy table?
Yes, of all good gifts the Giver
Thee we own,
Thee alone
Magnify for ever.

PART 2

3 Thankful for our every blessing,
Let us sing
Christ the Spring,
Never, never ceasing.
Source of all our gifts and graces
Christ we own,
Christ alone
Calls for all our praises.

4 He dispels our sin and sadness,
Life imparts,
Cheers our hearts,
Fills with food and gladness.
Who himself for all hath given
Us he feeds,
Us he leads
To a feast in heaven.

Charles Wesley (1707-88)

22

RUSTINGTON 87.87.D.

C. Hubert H. Parry (1848–1918)

1 God is Love: let heav'n a-dore him; God is Love: let earth re-joice;

Let cre - a-tion sing be-fore him, And ex - alt him with one voice.

He who laid the earth's foun - da-tion, He who spread the heav'ns a-bove,

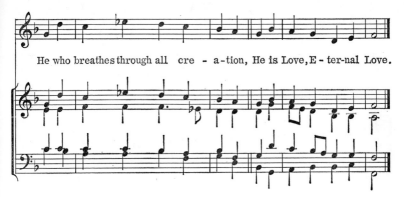

He who breathes through all cre - a-tion, He is Love, E - ter-nal Love.

Alternative Tune, ARFON, S.T.3.

God's Continuing Love

GOD is Love: let heav'n adore him;
　God is Love: let earth rejoice;
Let creation sing before him,
　And exalt him with one voice.
He who laid the earth's foundation,
　He who spread the heav'ns above,
He who breathes through all creation,
　He is Love, Eternal Love.

2 God is Love: and he enfoldeth
　All the world in one embrace;
With unfailing grasp he holdeth
　Every child of every race.
And when human hearts are breaking
　Under sorrow's iron rod,
Then they find that selfsame aching
　Deep within the heart of God.

3 God is Love: and though with blindness
　Sin afflicts the souls of men,
God's eternal loving-kindness
　Holds and guides them even then.
Sin and death and hell shall never
　O'er us final triumph gain;
God is Love, so Love for ever
　O'er the universe must reign.

Timothy Rees† (1874-1939)

NEW HORIZONS 77.77.77.
Unison

FRANCIS WESTBROOK (1903–)

1 God of con-crete, God of steel, God of pis-ton and of wheel,

God of py-lon, God of steam, God of gir-der and of beam,

God of a-tom, God of mine, All the world of power is thine!

'The Earth is the Lord's'

GOD of concrete, God of steel,
God of piston and of wheel,
God of pylon, God of steam,
God of girder and of beam,
God of atom, God of mine,
All the world of power is thine!

2 Lord of cable, Lord of rail,
Lord of motorway and mail,
Lord of rocket, Lord of flight,
Lord of soaring satellite,
Lord of lightning's livid line,
All the world of speed is thine!

3 Lord of science, Lord of art,
God of map and graph and chart,
Lord of physics and research,
Word of Bible, Faith of Church,
Lord of sequence and design,
All the world of truth is thine!

4 God whose glory fills the earth,
Gave the universe its birth,
Loosed the Christ with Easter's might,
Saves the world from evil's blight,
Claims mankind by grace divine,
ALL THE WORLD OF LOVE IS THINE!

Richard G. Jones (1926–   )

For Verse 4, line 3:

Loosed   the   Christ   with   Eas-ter's might,

24

OBIIT 87.87.87.   WALTER PARRATT (1841–1924)

1 God of grace and God of glo-ry, On thy peo-ple pour thy power;

Crown thine ancient Church's sto-ry; Bring her bud to glo-rious flower.

Grant us wis-dom, Grant us cour-age, For the fac-ing of this hour.

Alternative Tunes, GRAFTON, M.H.B. 93, and RHUDDLAN, M.H.B. 883
Music: © *Novello & Co. Ltd. Words:* © *H. E. Fosdick.*

A Prayer for Wisdom and Courage

GOD of grace and God of glory,
  On thy people pour thy power;
Crown thine ancient Church's story;
  Bring her bud to glorious flower.
      Grant us wisdom,
      Grant us courage,
  For the facing of this hour.

2 Lo! the hosts of evil round us
    Scorn thy Christ, assail his ways!
  Fears and doubts too long have bound us;
    Free our hearts to work and praise.
      Grant us wisdom,
      Grant us courage,
    For the living of these days.

3 Heal thy children's warring madness;
    Bend our pride to thy control;
  Shame our wanton, selfish gladness,
    Rich in things and poor in soul.
      Grant us wisdom,
      Grant us courage,
    Lest we miss thy kingdom's goal.

4 Set our feet on lofty places;
    Gird our lives that they may be
  Armoured with all Christ-like graces
    In the fight to set men free.
      Grant us wisdom,
      Grant us courage,
    That we fail not man nor thee.

H. E. Fosdick (1878-   )

25

BANGOR C.M.

Melody from W. TANS'UR'S *Compleat Melody* (1735)

For alternative harmonization, see M.H.B. 556

Science

GOD, who hast given us power to sound
Depths hitherto unknown:
To probe earth's hidden mysteries,
And make their might our own:

2 Great are thy gifts: yet greater far
This gift, O God, bestow,
That as to knowledge we attain
We may in wisdom grow.

3 Let wisdom's godly fear dispel
All fears that hate impart;
Give understanding to the mind,
And with new mind new heart.

4 So for thy glory and man's good
May we thy gifts employ,
Lest, maddened by the lust of power,
Man shall himself destroy.

G. W. Briggs (1875-1959)

It is suggested that this Hymn should end quietly and with deliberation.

Words: © *Oxford University Press.*

26

English Traditional Melody
Collected by LUCY BROADWOOD (1858–1929)
Harmonized and arranged by R. VAUGHAN WILLIAMS (1872–1958)

SHIPSTON 87.87.

God's Farm

GOD, whose farm is all creation,
   Take the gratitude we give;
Take the finest of our harvest,
   Crops we grow that men may live.

2 Take our ploughing, seeding, reaping,
   Hopes and fears of sun and rain,
All our thinking, planning, waiting,
   Ripened in this fruit and grain.

3 All our labour, all our watching,
   All our calendar of care,
In these crops of your creation,
   Take, O God: they are our prayer.

John Arlott (1914-   )

27

FIRST TUNE

KENSINGTON 87.87.87.   HERBERT HOWELLS (1892–   )

1 God who spoke in the be-gin-ning, form-ing rock and sha-ping
spar, set all life and growth in mo-tion, earth-y
world and dis-tant star; He who calls the earth to or-der

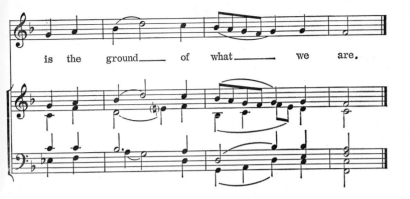

is the   ground____ of   what____   we   are.

The First and Final Word

GOD who spoke in the beginning,
    forming rock and shaping spar,
set all life and growth in motion,
    earthy world and distant star;
He who calls the earth to order
    is the ground of what we are.

2 God who spoke through men and nations,
    through events long past and gone;
showing still today his purpose,
    speaks supremely through his Son;
He who calls the earth to order
    gives his word and it is done.

3 God whose speech becomes incarnate,
    —Christ is servant, Christ is Lord!—
calls us to a life of service,
    heart and will to action stirred;
He who uses man's obedience
    has the first and final word.

Fred Kaan (1929-   )

Music: © *Novello & Co. Ltd. Words:* © *Fred Kaan.*

SECOND TUNE

SUMMERHILL 87.87.87.   IDA PRINS-EUTTLE (1908–   )

1 God who spoke in the be - gin - ning, form-ing rock and sha-ping spar, set all life and growth in mo-tion, earth-y world and dis-tant star; He who

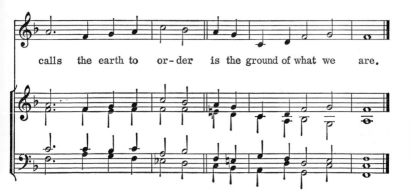

calls the earth to or-der is the ground of what we are.

The First and Final Word

GOD who spoke in the beginning,
    forming rock and shaping spar,
set all life and growth in motion,
    earthy world and distant star;
He who calls the earth to order
    is the ground of what we are.

2 God who spoke through men and nations,
    through events long past and gone;
showing still today his purpose,
    speaks supremely through his Son;
He who calls the earth to order
    gives his word and it is done.

3 God whose speech becomes incarnate,
    —Christ is servant, Christ is Lord!—
calls us to a life of service,
    heart and will to action stirred;
He who uses man's obedience
    has the first and final word.

Fred Kaan (1929-   )

28

LE P'ING 55.55.D.
('JOYOUS PEACE')

Chinese Melody by HU TE-AI (c.1900-)
Harmonized by BLISS WIANT (1895-)

1 Gold-en breaks the dawn,— Comes the east-ern sun,

O – ver lake and lawn— Set his course to run.

Birds a-bove us fly,— Flow-ers bloom be - low,

Through the earth and sky____ God's great mer-cies flow.

(It may be desirable to sing this tune a semitone higher)

God's Radiant Power

GOLDEN breaks the dawn,
Comes the eastern sun,
Over lake and lawn
Set his course to run.
Birds above us fly,
Flowers bloom below,
Through the earth and sky
God's great mercies flow.

2 Father God in heaven,
Hallowed be thy name,
Rule to thee be given,
Power and all acclaim.
Thee may we obey
As the hosts above,
Bread for us each day
Broken by thy love.

3 Pardoned, as we share
In thy pardoning power,
Kept from Satan's snare
In temptation's hour:
So from sin set free,
Lord, we seek thy face,
Sons of liberty,
Heirs of saving grace.

4 Grace to all men shown,
All that grace must know,
God, their Father, own,
To their Father go.
Christ will come at last,
Even now so near,
Night will soon be past
And the dawn appear.

Verse 1 from the Chinese of T. C. Chao (1888-   )
  Tr. Frank W. Price (1895-   )
Verses 2-4 by Daniel T. Niles (1908-   )

C

29

VULPIUS 888.4.
(GELOBT SEI GOTT)

Melody from M. VULPIUS's *Gesangbuch* (1609)
Harmonized by HENRY G. LEY (1887–1962)

Ped.

Harmony ad lib.

Al - le - lu - ia, Al - le - lu - ia, Al-le-lu - ia!

*From this point the following Descant may start: (j.w.)

Al - - le - lu - ia, Al - le - lu - ia, — Al-le - lu - ia!

The Life Restored

GOOD Christian men, rejoice and sing!
Now is the triumph of our King!
To all the world glad news we bring:
Alleluia!

2 The Lord of Life is risen for aye;
Bring flowers of song to strew his way;
Let all mankind rejoice and say:
Alleluia!

3 Praise we in songs of victory
That Love, that Life which cannot die,
And sing with hearts uplifted high:
Alleluia!

4 Thy name we bless, O risen Lord,
And sing today with one accord
The life laid down, the Life restored:
Alleluia!

C. A. Alington (1872-1955)

30

HAIL TO THE LORD 66.66.66. MALCOLM WILLIAMSON (1931–   )

Unison. *Rather quick*

1 Hail to the Lord who comes, Comes to his Tem — ple gate! Not with his an - gel host, Not in his king - ly state: No shouts pro - claim him nigh, No crowds his com — ing wait; —

Alternative Tune, OLD 120TH, M.H.B. 707

Music: © *J. Weinberger Ltd.*

The Presentation of Christ in the Temple

HAIL to the Lord who comes,
Comes to his Temple gate!
Not with his angel host,
Not in his kingly state:
No shouts proclaim him nigh,
No crowds his coming wait;

2 But borne upon the throne
Of Mary's gentle breast,
Watched by her duteous love,
In her fond arms at rest;
Thus to his Father's house
He comes, the heavenly Guest.

3 There Joseph at her side
In reverent wonder stands;
And, filled with holy joy,
Old Simeon in his hands
Takes up the promised Child,
The glory of all lands.

4 O Light of all the earth,
Thy children wait for thee:
Come to thy temples here,
That we, from sin set free,
Before thy Father's face
May all presented be.

J. Ellerton (1826-93)

31

ST ENODOC C.M.

C. S. LANG (1891–   )

1 Hast thou not known, hast thou not heard, That firm re-mains on high The ev-er-last—ing throne of him— Who formed the earth— and sky?

Alternative Tune, STRACATHRO, M.H.B. 102
Music: © *Novello & Co. Ltd.*

Isaiah 40. 28-31

H AST thou not known, hast thou not heard,
    That firm remains on high
The everlasting throne of him
    Who formed the earth and sky?

2 Art thou afraid his power shall fail
    When comes thy evil day?
And can an all-creating arm
    Grow weary or decay?

3 Supreme in wisdom as in power
    The Rock of Ages stands;
Though him thou canst not see, nor trace
    The working of his hands.

4 He gives the conquest to the weak,
    Supports the fainting heart;
And courage in the evil hour
    His heavenly aids impart.

5 Mere human power shall fast decay,
    And youthful vigour cease;
But they who wait upon the Lord
    In strength shall still increase.

Scottish Paraphrases (1781)
partly based on Isaac Watts

32

TWIGWORTH 87.87.D.

HERBERT HOWELLS (1892–)

1 Holy Spirit, ever dwelling In the holiest realms of light;

Holy Spirit, ever brooding O'er a world of gloom and night;

Holy Spirit, ever raising Sons of earth to thrones on high;

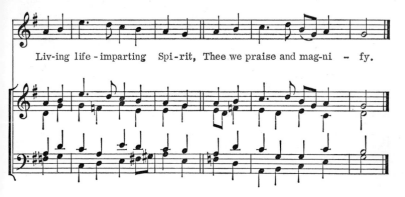

Liv-ing life - imparting Spi-rit, Thee we praise and mag-ni - fy.

Alternative Tunes, ADRIAN, M.H.B. 898; ABBOT'S LEIGH, NO. 42

Praise to the Holy Spirit

HOLY Spirit, ever dwelling
In the holiest realms of light;
Holy Spirit, ever brooding
O'er a world of gloom and night;
Holy Spirit, ever raising
Sons of earth to thrones on high;
Living, life-imparting Spirit,
Thee we praise and magnify.

2 Holy Spirit, ever living
As the Church's very life;
Holy Spirit, ever striving
Through her in a ceaseless strife;
Holy Spirit, ever forming
In the Church the mind of Christ;
Thee we praise with endless worship
For thy fruit and gifts unpriced.

3 Holy Spirit, ever working
Through the Church's ministry;
Quickening, strengthening, and absolving,
Setting captive sinners free;
Holy Spirit, ever binding
Age to age, and soul to soul,
In a fellowship unending—
Thee we worship and extol.

Timothy Rees (1874-1939)

33

Melody by P. Nicolai (1556–1608)

WIE SCHÖN LEUCHTET 887.887.4848. Harmony adapted from Bach and Mendelssohn

1 How bright-ly shines the Morn-ing Star! The na-tions see and hail a-far

The Light in Ju-dah shin - ing. Thou Da-vid's son of Ja-cob's race,

The Bride-groom, and the King of grace, For thee our hearts are

pin - ing! Low-ly, ho - ly, Great and glor-ious, thou vic-tor-ious

Prince of gra - ces, Fill-ing all the heav'n-ly pla - ces!

Christ, the Morning Star

Wie schön leuchtet der Morgenstern

HOW brightly shines the Morning Star!
The nations see and hail afar
    The Light in Judah shining.
Thou David's son of Jacob's race,
The Bridegroom, and the King of grace,
    For thee our hearts are pining!
        Lowly, holy,
Great and glorious, thou victorious
        Prince of graces,
Filling all the heavenly places!

2 Though circled by the hosts on high,
He deigns to cast a pitying eye
    Upon his helpless creature;
The whole Creation's Head and Lord,
By highest seraphim adored,
    Assumes our very nature.
        Jesu, grant us,
Through thy merit, to inherit
        Thy salvation;
Hear, O hear our supplication.

3 Rejoice, ye heav'ns; thou earth, reply;
With praise, ye sinners, fill the sky,
    For this his Incarnation.
Incarnate God, put forth thy power,
Ride on, ride on, great Conqueror,
    Till all know thy salvation.
        Amen, Amen!
Alleluia, Alleluia!
        Praise be given
Evermore by earth and heaven.

P. Nicolai (1556-1608)
Tr. H. Harbaugh† (1860) *and W. Mercer†* (1859)

34

McKEE C.M.

With dignity.   May be sung in Unison

Negro Melody, adapted by
HARRY T. BURLEIGH (1866–1946)

(For singing in harmony the key of C may be preferable.)

Brotherhood in Christ

IN Christ there is no East or West,
 In him no South or North,
But one great fellowship of love
 Throughout the whole wide earth.

2 In him shall true hearts everywhere
 Their high communion find,
His service is the golden cord
 Close-binding all mankind.

3 Join hands, then, brothers of the faith,
 Whate'er your race may be;
Who serves my Father as a son
 Is surely kin to me.

4 In Christ now meet both East and West,
 In him meet South and North,
All Christlike souls are one in him,
 Throughout the whole wide earth.

John Oxenham† (1852-1941)

Words: © Theodora & Roderic Dunkerley.

35

WILLIAM H. HARRIS (1883–)

Alternative Tune, DA CHRISTUS GEBOREN WAR, M.H.B. 810

Looking unto Jesus

JESUS, Lord, we look to thee,
Let us in thy name agree;
Show thyself the Prince of Peace;
Bid our jarring conflicts cease.

2 By thy reconciling love,
Every stumbling-block remove;
Each to each unite, endear;
Come, and spread thy banner here.

3 Make us of one heart and mind,
Courteous, pitiful, and kind,
Lowly, meek in thought and word,
Altogether like our Lord.

4 Let us for each other care,
Each the other's burden bear,
To thy Church the pattern give,
Show how true believers live.

5 Free from anger and from pride,
Let us thus in God abide;
All the depths of love express,
All the height of holiness.

Charles Wesley† (1707-88)

36

ARTHUR SOMERVELL (1863–1937)
(From *The Passion of Christ*)

Alternative Tune, REDHEAD NO. 66, M.H.B. 160

On relieving Christ in the Poor

JESUS, my Lord, how rich thy grace,
Thy bounties how complete!
How shall I count the matchless sum?
How pay the mighty debt?

2 High on a throne of radiant light
Dost thou exalted shine;
What can my poverty bestow
When all the worlds are thine?

3 But thou hast brethren here below,
The partners of thy grace,
And wilt confess their humble names
Before thy Father's face.

4 In them thou may'st be clothed and fed,
And visited and cheered,
And in their accents of distress
My Saviour's voice is heard.

5 Thy face with reverence and with love
I in thy poor would see;
O let me rather beg my bread
Than hold it back from thee.

Philip Doddridge (1702-51)

37

ST BRIDE S.M.

SAMUEL HOWARD (1710–82)
(Harmony altered in first line)

For alternative harmonization, see M.H.B. 81.

Following Jesus

JESU, we follow thee,
In all thy footsteps tread,
And seek for full conformity
To our exalted Head.

2   We would, we would partake
Thy every state below,
And suffer all things for thy sake,
And to thy glory go.

3   We in thy birth are born,
Sustain thy grief and loss,
Share in thy want, and shame, and scorn,
And die upon thy Cross.

4   Baptized into thy death
We sink into thy grave,
Till thou the quick'ning spirit breathe,
And to the utmost save.

5   Thou saidst, 'Where'er I am,
There shall my servants be'.
Master, the welcome word we claim,
And die to live with thee.

6   To us who share thy pain,
Thy joy shall soon be given,
And we shall in thy glory reign,
For thou art now in heaven.

Charles Wesley† (1707-88)

38

PICARDY 87.87.87.
Unison

French Carol Melody, as harmonized
in *The English Hymnal* (1906)

ALTERNATIVE HARMONY VERSION

Harmonized by FRANCIS WESTBROOK (1903–   )

King of Kings, yet born of Mary

Σιγησάτω πᾶσα σὰρξ βροτεία

LET all mortal flesh keep silence, and with fear and trembling stand;
Ponder nothing earthly-minded, for with blessing in his hand
Christ our God to earth descendeth, our full homage to demand.

2 King of Kings, yet born of Mary, as of old on earth he stood,
Lord of Lords, in human vesture—in the body and the blood—
He will give to all the faithful his own self for heav'nly food.

3 Rank on rank the host of heaven spreads its vanguard on the way,
As the Light of Light descendeth from the realms of endless day,
That the powers of hell may vanish as the darkness clears away.

4 At his feet the six-winged seraph; cherubim with sleepless eye
Veil their faces to the Presence, as with ceaseless voice they cry—
Alleluia, Alleluia, Alleluia, Lord most high!

From the Liturgy of St James
Tr. G. Moultrie (1829-85)

This hymn was used in Eastern Churches in the 5th century or earlier, at the place in the Eucharist corresponding to the Offertory in the Western Church.

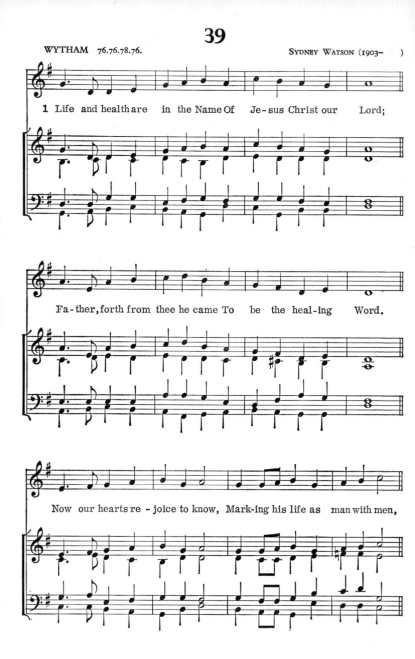

39

WYTHAM   76.76.78.76.   SYDNEY WATSON (1903–   )

1 Life and health are in the Name Of Je-sus Christ our Lord;

Fa-ther, forth from thee he came To be the heal-ing Word.

Now our hearts re-joice to know, Mark-ing his life as man with men,

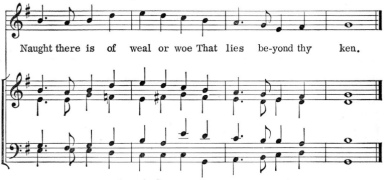

Naught there is of weal or woe That lies be-yond thy ken.

Alternative Tune, AMSTERDAM, M.H.B. 17

The Healing Word

LIFE and health are in the Name
Of Jesus Christ our Lord:
Father, forth from thee he came
To be the healing Word.
Now our hearts rejoice to know,
Marking his life as man with men,
Naught there is of weal or woe
That lies beyond thy ken.

2 Thine the gift of patient will,
Affliction to endure;
Thine the gift of eager skill
That toils to find a cure.
Art to quell the fever's rage,
Faith in the potency of prayer,
Knowledge gained from age to age,
Are tokens of thy care.

3 Teach us how to use aright
These bounties of thy grace,
Bringing sweetness, health, and light
In every stricken place.
May on earth thy kingdom grow,
Knowledge and faith have common aim,
And the fruits of mercy show
The splendour of thy name.

J. R. Darbyshire (1880-1948)

Music: © Sydney Watson. Words: © C. R. Darbyshire.

40

CRUCIFER 10 10 & Refrain

S. H. NICHOLSON (1875–1947)

Verse 1. Unison (to be repeated as a Refrain)

1 Lift high the Cross, the love of Christ pro - claim

Till all the world____ a - dore____ his sa - cred name.

Fine

Verses 2-7. Harmony

D.C.

Org.

The Victory of the Cross

*L*IFT *high the Cross, the love of Christ proclaim*
Till all the world adore his sacred name.

2 Come, brethren, follow where our Captain trod,
Our King victorious, Christ the Son of God:

3 Led on their way by this triumphant sign,
The hosts of God in conquering ranks combine:

4 Each new-born soldier of the Crucified
Bears on his brow the seal of him who died:

5 From north and south, from east and west they raise
In growing unison their song of praise:

6 O Lord, once lifted on the glorious Tree,
As thou hast promised, draw men unto thee:

7 From farthest regions let them homage bring,
And on his Cross adore their Saviour King:

M. R. Newbolt (1874-1956)
based on G. W. Kitchin (1827-1912)

41

FONT 88.87.   STANLEY MOUNTFORD (1902–   )

1 Lord, here is one to be bap-tized, Not know-ing how or when or where— Too fresh on earth to be sur-prised By a hid-den cos-mic care.

Baptismal Hymn

LORD, here is one to be baptized,
Not knowing how or when or where—
Too fresh on earth to be surprised
    By a hidden cosmic care.

2 You, Lord, in Jordan were immersed,
One flesh with every child of Cain:
Earth's angry children fret and thirst
    Until justice falls like rain.

3 So at the font transcend our songs,
Give us the sign of things made new:
'New earth' is where this child belongs,
    Who belongs, earth's Goal, to you.

4 Yours the new Church by water born,
Strong for all families on earth.
Our deadness, not your death, we mourn,
    As you bring fresh hope to birth.

5 High our surprise at what you do,
Calling our race from tomb of death.
Lord, here is faith and water too—
    Here is one to take deep Breath.

David Head (1922-   )

Music: © *S. Mountford. Words:* ©. *D. H. G. Head.*

42

CYRIL V. TAYLOR (1907–   )

Missionary Hymn

LORD, thy Church on earth is seeking
　Thy renewal from above:
Teach us all the art of speaking
　With the accent of thy love.
We would heed thy great commission:
　Go ye into every place—
Preach, baptize, fulfil my mission,
　Serve with love and share my grace.

2 Freedom give to those in bondage,
　Lift the burdens caused by sin.
Give new hope, new strength and courage,
　Grant release from fears within:
Light for darkness; joy for sorrow;
　Love for hatred; peace for strife.
These and countless blessings follow
　As the Spirit gives new life.

3 In the streets of every city
　Where the bruised and lonely dwell,
We shall show the Saviour's pity,
　We shall of his mercy tell.
In all lands and with all races
　We shall serve, and seek to bring
All mankind to render praises,
　Christ, to thee, Redeemer, King.

Hugh Sherlock (1905-　　)

43
FIRST TUNE

MAY HILL 87.87.

SYDNEY WATSON (1903–

Desiring to be One in Christ

Lass den Brüdern uns begegnen

LORD, we long to join our brethren
whom our rival laws restrain,
But who study just as we do
Christ's own standards to maintain.

2 Lord, we long to share their worship
who prefer another form,
But whose anthems, just as ours do,
take Christ's glory as their norm.

3 Lord, we long to stand beside them
in fulfilment of your plan
That by true faith shall your kingdom
bring reality to man.

4 For our church is not your kingdom:
this your word may teach us still.
No, your kingdom, Lord, is greater:
reconcile us in your will.

Otmar Schulz (1938-   )
Tr. Ivor H. Jones (1934-   )

Music: © *Sydney Watson.*

LASS DEN BRÜDERN 87.87.   ROLF SCHWEIZER (1967)

Unison.   Not too fast

1 Lord, we long to join our breth-ren   whom our ri-val laws   re - strain,

But who stu - dy just as we do Christ's own standards to   main-tain.

The original German hymn, and the tune above, are from the 1967 Hanover Kirchentag.

The accompaniment is for organ, with optional string bass duplicating the pedal part, and with the following additional part for vibraphone or other solo instrument:

44

IVINGHOE 87.87.D.

GREVILLE COOKE (1894–)

1 Lord, whose love in hum-ble ser-vice Bore the weight of hu-man need,

Who didst on the Cross, for-sa-ken, Work thy mer-cy's per-fect deed:

small notes Organ only

We, thy ser-vants, bring the wor-ship Not of voice a – lone, but heart;

Con - se - cra - ting   to thy pur-pose Ev-ery gift thou   dost im-part.

Alternative Tune, BETHANY, M.H.B. 800

The Greatness of Service

LORD, whose love in humble service
　Bore the weight of human need,
Who didst on the Cross, forsaken,
　Work thy mercy's perfect deed:
We, thy servants, bring the worship
　Not of voice alone, but heart;
Consecrating to thy purpose
　Every gift thou dost impart.

2 As we worship, grant us vision,
　Till thy love's revealing light,
In its height and depth and greatness,
　Dawns upon our quickened sight;
Making known the needs and burdens
　Thy compassion bids us bear,
Stirring us to tireless striving
　Thine abundant life to share.

3 Called from worship unto service
　Forth in thy dear name we go,
To the child, the youth, the aged,
　Love in living deeds to show.
Hope and health, goodwill and comfort,
　Counsel, aid and peace we give,
That thy children, Lord, in freedom
　May thy mercy know, and live.

Albert F. Bayly (1901-　　)

Music: © Galliard Ltd. Words: © Albert F. Bayly.

45

GOTT DES HIMMELS 87.87.

Adapted by C. STEGGALL (1826–1905)
from J. S. BACH's setting of a melody
by H. ALBERT (1604–51)

'*Now unto Him . . .*'

MAY the grace of Christ our Saviour,
  And the Father's boundless love,
With the Holy Spirit's favour,
  Rest upon us from above.

2 Thus may we abide in union
  With each other and the Lord,
And possess, in sweet communion,
  Joys which earth cannot afford.

John Newton (1725-1807)

46

WOODBRIDGE ROAD L.M. JOHN WILSON (1905–)

(For singing in harmony the keys of F sharp or G are preferable).
Alternative Tune, EISENACH, M.H.B. 47

The Lord's Supper

MY God, and is thy table spread?
And does thy cup with love o'erflow?
Thither be all thy children led
And let them all its sweetness know.

2 Hail, sacred feast, which Jesus makes,
Rich banquet of his flesh and blood!
Thrice happy he, who here partakes
That sacred stream, that heavenly food!

3 O let thy table honoured be,
And furnished well with joyful guests;
And may each soul salvation see,
That here its sacred pledges tastes. *Amen.*

Philip Doddridge (1702–51)

47

ST BARTHOLOMEW L.M.

HENRY DUNCALF (18th century)
from W. RILEY's *Parochial Harmony*, 1762

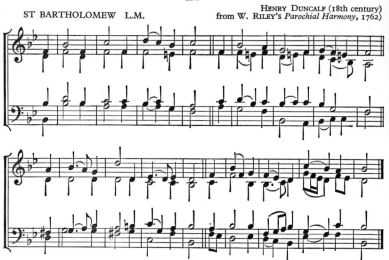

For alternative harmonization, see M.H.B. 895.

The Greatness of God

MY God, my King, thy various praise
Shall fill the remnant of my days;
Thy grace employ my humble tongue,
Till death and glory raise the song.

2 The wings of every hour shall bear
Some thankful tribute to thine ear,
And every setting sun shall see
New works of duty done for thee.

3 Thy truth and justice I'll proclaim;
Thy bounty flows, an endless stream;
Thy mercy swift; thine anger slow,
But dreadful to the stubborn foe.

4 Let distant times and nations raise
The long succession of thy praise;
And unborn ages make my song
The joy and labour of their tongue.

5 But who can speak thy wondrous deeds?
Thy greatness all our thoughts exceeds;
Vast and unsearchable thy ways,
Vast and immortal be thy praise.

Isaac Watts (1674-1748)
based on Psalm 145

48

From an original hymn-tune by J. S. BACH (1685–1750)
Adapted by JOHN WILSON (1905–   )

NÜRNBERG L.M.

Christ Crucified; The Wisdom and Power of God

NATURE with open volume stands
To spread her Maker's praise abroad,
And every labour of his hands
Shows something worthy of a God.

2 But in the grace that rescued man
His brightest form of glory shines;
Here on the Cross 'tis fairest drawn
In precious blood and crimson lines.

3 Here his whole Name appears complete;
Nor wit can guess, nor reason prove
Which of the letters best is writ,
The Power, the Wisdom, or the Love.

4 O the sweet wonders of that Cross
Where God the Saviour loved and died!
Her noblest life my spirit draws
From his dear wounds and bleeding side.

5 I would for ever speak his Name
In sounds to mortal ears unknown,
With angels join to praise the Lamb,
And worship at his Father's throne.

Isaac Watts (1674-1748)

D

49

MANNA 886.886.

Melody, and most of the harmony,
by J. G. SCHICHT (1753–1823)

1 Not far be-yond the sea nor high A - bove the heav'ns, but

ve - ry nigh Thy voice, O God, is heard. For

each new step of faith we take Thou hast more truth and

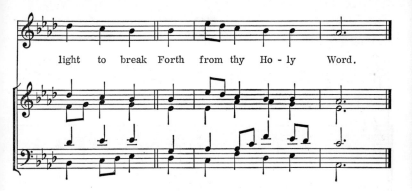

light   to   break   Forth   from thy   Ho - ly   Word.

Truth and Light from Scripture

NOT far beyond the sea nor high
Above the heavens, but very nigh
    Thy voice, O God, is heard.
For each new step of faith we take
Thou hast more truth and light to break
    Forth from thy Holy Word.

2 The babe in Christ thy Scriptures feed
With milk sufficient for his need,
    The nurture of the Lord.
Beneath life's burden and its heat
The full-grown man finds stronger meat
    In thy unfailing Word.

3 Rooted and grounded in thy love,
With saints on earth and saints above
    We join in full accord,
To grasp the breadth, length, depth, and height,
The crucified and risen might
    Of Christ, the Incarnate Word.

4 Help us to press toward that mark,
And, though our vision now is dark,
    To live by what we see.
So, when we see thee face to face,
Thy truth and light our dwelling-place
    For evermore shall be.

G. B. Caird (1917-   )

50

NIAGARA L.M.

R. JACKSON (1840–1914)

1 Now let us from this ta–ble rise re-newed in bo-dy, mind and soul; with Christ we die and live a-gain, his self-less love has made us whole.

The Sacrament of Care

Now let us from this table rise
renewed in body, mind and soul;
with Christ we die and live again,
his selfless love has made us whole.

2 With minds alert, upheld by grace,
to spread the Word in speech and deed,
we follow in the steps of Christ,
at one with man in hope and need.

3 To fill each human house with love,
it is the sacrament of care;
the work that Christ began to do
we humbly pledge ourselves to share.

4 Then give us courage, Father God,
to choose again the pilgrim way,
and help us to accept with joy
the challenge of tomorrow's day.

Fred Kaan (1929-   )

51

INVITATION L.M.

Later form of a tune by J. F. LAMPE (1703–51)
mostly as in *The Temple Church Choral Service Book*, 1880

A Prayer for Wholeness

O CHRIST, the Healer, we have come
To pray for health, to plead for friends.
How can we fail to be restored,
When reached by love that never ends?

2 From every ailment flesh endures
Our bodies clamour to be freed;
Yet in our hearts we would confess
That wholeness is our deepest need.

3 How strong, O Lord, are our desires,
How weak our knowledge of ourselves!
Release in us those healing truths
Unconscious pride resists and shelves.

4 In conflicts that destroy our health
We diagnose the world's disease;
Our common life declares our ills:
Is there no cure, O Christ, for these?

5 Grant that we all, made one in faith,
In your community may find
The wholeness that, enriching us,
Shall reach and shall enrich mankind.

F. Pratt Green (1903–   )

INVITATION L.M.
Unison

Melody and figured bass
by J. F. LAMPE (1703–51)

1 O Christ, the Heal - er, we have come To pray for health, to___ plead for friends. How can we fail to be res-tored, When reached by love that ne - ver ends?

52

FIRST TUNE

FOSTER S.M.

M. B. FOSTER (1851–1922)

ALTERNATIVE HARMONIZATION FOR VERSE 5

Choir and Organ.   Congregation sing melody as above.

Version from
The Clarendon Hymn Book (1936)

HILLSBOROUGH S.M.   JOHN GARDNER (1917–   )

A Prayer for God's Kingdom

O DAY of God, draw nigh
In beauty and in power,
Come with thy timeless judgment now
To match our present hour.

2   Bring to our troubled minds,
Uncertain and afraid,
The quiet of a steadfast faith,
Calm of a call obeyed.

3   Bring justice to our land,
That all may dwell secure,
And finely build for days to come
Foundations that endure.

4   Bring to our world of strife
Thy sovereign word of peace,
That war may haunt the earth no more
And desolation cease.

5   O Day of God, draw nigh
As at creation's birth;
Let there be light again, and set
Thy judgments in the earth.

R. B. Y. Scott (1899–   )

53

FRANCIS WESTBROOK (1903–   )

The Cross in our Life

O DEAREST Lord, thy sacred head
With thorns was pierced for me;
O pour thy blessing on my head,
That I may think for thee.

2 O dearest Lord, thy sacred hands
With nails were pierced for me;
O shed thy blessing on my hands,
That they may work for thee.

3 O dearest Lord, thy sacred feet
With nails were pierced for me;
O pour thy blessing on my feet,
That they may follow thee.

4 O dearest Lord, thy sacred heart
With spear was pierced for me;
O pour thy spirit in my heart,
That I may live for thee.

Father Andrew (H. E. Hardy) (1869–1946)

54

Melody attributed to W. TURNER (1651–1740)
Harmonized by S. S. WESLEY (1810–76)

EGHAM S.M.

Of such is the Kingdom . . .

O FATHER who didst give
In Jesus Christ thy Son
A Saviour for each child of earth—
We bring our little one.

2 For thou in tenderness
Beyond all human care
Stooping to save the least, hast said
That such thy Kingdom share.

3 And we have known thy grace,
Creator, Healer, Friend;
Thy constant love enriches ours:
We on thy might depend.

4 So now in joyful trust
Facing the years to be,
Our child, our daily life, ourselves
We dedicate to thee.

5 O may thy wisdom lead;
Our strength be thine alone,
Until the faith we now confess
Thy child shall make *his* own.

6 Here in this sacrament,
Joined with our friends above,
In Christ's one church we yield *him* now
To thine unchanging love.

R. A. Bethel (1910–46)

55

RYBURN 88.88.88.

NORMAN COCKER (1889–1953)

1 O Fa-ther, whose cre - a – ting hand
Brings har-vest from the fruit-ful land,
Thy pro-vi-dence we glad – ly own
And bring our hymns be -fore thy throne
To praise thee for the

liv - ing bread   On which our lives are dai - ly fed.

Freely ye have received . . .

O FATHER, whose creating hand
Brings harvest from the fruitful land,
Thy providence we gladly own
And bring our hymns before thy throne
To praise thee for the living bread
On which our lives are daily fed.

2 Lord, who didst in the desert feed
The hungry thousands in their need,
Where want and famine still abound
Let thy relieving love be found,
And in thy name may we supply
Thy hungry children when they cry.

3 O Spirit, thy revealing light
Has led our questing souls aright;
Source of our science, who hast taught
The marvels human minds have wrought,
So that the barren deserts yield
The bounty by thy love revealed.

Donald Hughes (1911-67)

56

RERUM CREATOR 11 10.11 10.
Unison. Moving easily

JOHN WILSON (1905–)

1 O Lord of ev - ery shi - ning con - stel - la - tion That

wheels in splen-dour through the mid-night sky; Grant

us your Spi-rit's true il - lu - mi - na - tion To read the se-crets

Verses 1-4 | *Verse 5*
of your work on high. im – mor – tal – i – ty.

Verses 1-4 | *Verse 5*

allarg.

Alternative Tune, ZU MEINEM HERRN, M.H.B. 577

'Wisdom and Might are His'

O LORD of every shining constellation
    That wheels in splendour through the midnight sky;
Grant us your Spirit's true illumination
    To read the secrets of your work on high.

2 You, Lord, have made the atom's hidden forces,
    Your laws its mighty energies fulfil;
Teach us, to whom you give such rich resources,
    In all we use, to serve your holy will.

3 O Life, awaking life in cell and tissue,
    From flower to bird, from beast to brain of man;
Help us to trace, from birth to final issue,
    The sure unfolding of your age-long plan.

4 You, Lord, have stamped your image on your creatures,
    And, though they mar that image, love them still;
Lift up our eyes to Christ, that in his features
    We may discern the beauty of your will.

5 Great Lord of nature, shaping and renewing,
    You made us more than nature's sons to be;
You help us tread, with grace our souls enduing,
    The road to life and immortality.

Albert F. Bayly (1901–   )

57

WINCHESTER NEW   L.M.

Adapted from a tune in
Musicalisch Hand-Buch (Hamburg, 1690)

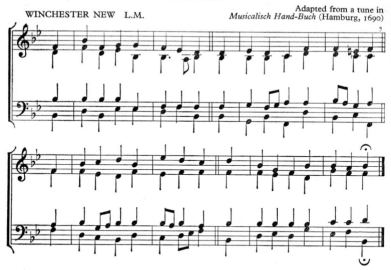

Preparing for Christ

Jordanis oras praevia

ON Jordan's bank the Baptist's cry
Announces that the Lord is nigh;
Awake and hearken, for he brings
Glad tidings from the King of Kings.

2 Then cleansed be every Christian breast,
And furnished for so great a guest!
Yea, let us each our hearts prepare
For Christ to come and enter there.

3 For thou art our salvation, Lord,
Our refuge, and our great reward;
Without thy grace we waste away
Like flowers that wither and decay.

4 To heal the sick stretch out thine hand,
And bid the fallen sinner stand;
Shine forth, and let thy light restore
Earth's own true loveliness once more.

5 All praise, eternal Son, to thee
Whose advent sets thy people free,
Whom, with the Father, we adore,
And Holy Ghost, for evermore.

C. Coffin (1676-1749)
Tr. J. Chandler (1806-76) *and others*

SOLEMNIS HAEC FESTIVITAS L.M.

Melody from *Paris Gradual* (1685)

Unison. Flowing easily

1 On Jor - dan's bank the Bap - tist's cry An -
noun-ces that the Lord is nigh; A - wake and heark-en,
for— he brings Glad ti - dings from— the King of Kings.

58

ST BOTOLPH C.M.

GORDON SLATER (1896–)

Alternative Tune, KILMARNOCK, M.H.B. 108

'Open our eyes'

O THOU who this mysterious bread
   Didst in Emmaus break,
Return herewith our souls to feed,
   And to thy followers speak.

2 Unseal the volume of thy grace,
   Apply the gospel word,
Open our eyes to see thy face,
   Our hearts to know the Lord.

3 Of thee we còmmune still, and mourn
   Till thou the veil remove,
Talk with us, and our hearts shall burn
   With flames of fervent love.

4 Inkindle now the heav'nly zeal,
   And make thy mercy known,
And give our pard'ning souls to feel
   That God and love are one.

Charles Wesley (1707-88)

59

CONTEMPLATION C.M. F. A. GORE OUSELEY (1825–89)

Alternative Tune, ST HUGH, M.H.B. 103

For Young Parents

OUR Father, whose creative love
The gift of life bestows,
Each child of earthly union born
Thy heav'nly likeness shows.

2 Grant those entrusted with the care
Of precious life from thee,
Thy grace, that worthy of the gift
And faithful they may be.

3 Teach them to meet the growing needs
Of infant, child and youth;
To build the body, train the mind
To know and love the truth:

4 And, highest task, to feed the soul
With Christ, the living Bread;
That each unfolding life may grow
Strong in thy paths to tread.

5 These parents need thy wisdom's light,
Thy love within their heart;
Bless thou their home, and, for their task,
Thy Spirit's grace impart.

Albert F. Bayly (1901-   )

60

First Tune

Second Tune

FRANCONIA S.M.

W. H. HAVERGAL (1793–1870), adapted from a tune
in KÖNIG'S *Harmonischer Lieder-Schatz* (1738)
(harmony slightly altered)

For this tune in a higher key, see M.H.B. 690.

The Annunciation

PRAISE we the Lord this day,
This day so long foretold,
Whose promise shone with cheering ray
On waiting saints of old.

2　The prophet gave the sign
For faithful men to read:
A Virgin, born of David's line,
Shall bear the promised Seed.

3　Ask not how this should be,
But worship and adore;
Like her, whom heaven's majesty
Came down to shadow o'er.

4　Meekly she bowed her head
To hear the gracious word,
Mary, the pure and lowly maid,
The favoured of the Lord.

5　Blessèd shall be her name
In all the Church on earth,
Through whom that wondrous mercy came,
The incarnate Saviour's birth.

Anonymous† (1846)

61

Melody from *Scottish Psalter* (1615)
Harmony adapted from J. MILTON (senior) in
RAVENSCROFT's *Psalmes* (1621)

YORK C.M.

For Alternative Version, see M.H.B. 347.

The Household of Faith

PRAY that Jerusalem may have
  Peace and felicity:
Let them that love thee and thy peace
  Have still prosperity.

2 Behold how good a thing it is,
  And how becoming well,
Together such as brethren are
  In unity to dwell.

3 Therefore I wish that peace may still
  Within thy walls remain,
And ever may thy palaces
  Prosperity retain.

4 Now, for my friends' and brethren's sake,
  Peace be in thee, I'll say;
And for the house of God our Lord
  I'll seek thy good alway.

Scottish Psalter (1650)
From Psalm 122. 6-9 and Psalm 133. 1

62

CHRISTCHURCH 66.66.88.   C. STEGGALL (1826–1905)

For this tune in altered rhythm, see M.H.B. 653.

Christ and His Church are One

SEE where our great High-Priest
Before the Lord appears,
And on his loving breast
The tribes of Israel bears,
Never without his people seen,
The Head of all believing men!

2 With him the corner stone
The living stones conjoin;
Christ and his church are one,
One body and one vine;
For us he uses all his powers,
And all he has, or is, is ours.

3 The promptings of our Head
The members all pursue,
By his good spirit led
To act and suffer too;
Whate'er he did on earth sustain,
Till glorious all like him we reign.

Charles Wesley† (1707-88)

63 First Version

PANGE LINGUA 87.87.87.

Unison

Plainsong Melody (Sarum form), Mode iii

1 Sing, my tongue, the Saviour's glory, Of his flesh the mystery sing;—

Of the blood, all price exceeding, Shed by our immortal King,—

God made man for man's salvation His own self now offering.

A - men.

The Last Supper

Pange lingua gloriosi corporis mysterium

SING, my tongue, the Saviour's glory,
  Of his flesh the mystery sing;
Of the blood, all price exceeding,
  Shed by our immortal King,
God made man for man's salvation
  His own self now offering.

2 Born for us, and for us given,
  Born a man like us below,
He, as man with men abiding,
  Dwelt, the seeds of truth to sow;
And at last faced death undaunted,
  Thus his greatest deed to show.

3 On the night of that Last Supper
  Seated with his chosen band,
He, the paschal victim eating,
  First fulfils the Law's command,
Then as food to all his brethren
  Gives himself with his own hand.

4 Therefore we before him falling
  This great sacrament revere;
Ancient forms are now departed,
  For new acts of grace are here;
Faith, our feeble senses aiding,
  Makes the Saviour's presence clear.

5 To the everlasting Father,
  And the Son who reigns on high,
With the Holy Ghost proceeding
  Forth from each eternally,
Be salvation, honour, blessing,
  Might, and endless majesty.
      Amen.

*St Thomas Aquinas (c. 1225-74)
Tr. E. Caswall (1814-78) and others*

63 *(continued)*

SECOND VERSION

PANGE LINGUA   87.87.87
Unison

Plainsong Melody (Sarum form) Mode iii
Harmonized by CHARLES WOOD (1866–1926),
in his *Passion According to St Mark*

A - men.

The Last Supper

Pange lingua gloriosi corporis mysterium

S ING, my tongue, the Saviour's glory,
    Of his flesh the mystery sing;
Of the blood, all price exceeding,
    Shed by our immortal King,
God made man for man's salvation
    His own self now offering.

2 Born for us, and for us given,
    Born a man like us below,
He, as man with men abiding,
    Dwelt, the seeds of truth to sow;
And at last faced death undaunted,
    Thus his greatest deed to show.

3 On the night of that Last Supper
    Seated with his chosen band,
He, the paschal victim eating,
    First fulfils the Law's command,
Then as food to all his brethren
    Gives himself with his own hand.

4 Therefore we before him falling
    This great sacrament revere;
Ancient forms are now departed,
    For new acts of grace are here;
Faith, our feeble senses aiding,
    Makes the Saviour's presence clear.

5 To the everlasting Father,
    And the Son who reigns on high,
With the Holy Ghost proceeding
    Forth from each eternally,
Be salvation, honour, blessing,
    Might, and endless majesty.
                            Amen.

St Thomas Aquinas (c. 1225-74)
Tr. E. Caswall (1814-78) and others

64
FIRST TUNE

NORTHAMPTON 77.77·

C. J. KING (1859–1934)

Glory to God in the Highest

SONGS of praise the angels sang,
Heaven with alleluias rang,
When Jehovah's work begun,
When he spake, and it was done.

2 Songs of praise awoke the morn
When the Prince of Peace was born;
Songs of praise arose when he
Captive led captivity.

3 Heaven and earth must pass away,
Songs of praise shall crown that day;
God will make new heavens, new earth,
Songs of praise shall hail their birth.

4 And will man alone be dumb
Till that glorious kingdom come?
No! the Church delights to raise
Psalms and hymns and songs of praise.

5 Saints below, with heart and voice,
Still in songs of praise rejoice,
Learning here, by faith and love,
Songs of praise to sing above.

6 Borne upon their latest breath,
Songs of praise shall conquer death;
Then, amidst eternal joy,
Songs of praise their powers employ.

James Montgomery (1771–1854)

Music: © Proprietors of Hymns Ancient and Modern

LAUDS 77.77.

JOHN WILSON (1905–)

Flowing easily.

1 Songs of praise the an-gels sang, Heav'n with al - le - lu - ias rang.

When Je-ho-vah's work be-gun, When he spake, and it was done.

(Small notes organ only)

(It may be desirable to sing this tune a semitone higher.)

OPTIONAL DESCANT FOR VERSES 3 AND 6

Sopranos. (Other voices sing unison melody).

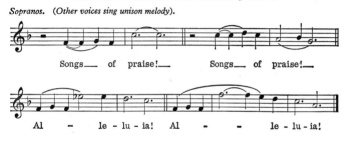

Songs— of praise!— Songs— of praise!—

Al – le - lu - ia! Al – – le - lu - ia!

Music: © Oxford University Press

65

CROSSINGS 89.89.D.

C. ARMSTRONG GIBBS (1889–1960)

Unison. In moderate time

Desiring God

THEE will I love, my God and King,
Thee will I sing, my strength and tower:
For evermore thee will I trust,
O God most just of truth and power:
Who all things hast in order placed,
Yea, for thy pleasure hast created;
And on thy throne unseen, unknown,
Reignest alone in glory seated.

2   Set in my heart thy love I find;
My wand'ring mind to thee thou leadest;
My trembling hope, my strong desire
With heav'nly fire thou kindly feedest.
Lo, all things fair thy path prepare,
Thy beauty to my spirit calleth,
Thine to remain in joy or pain,
And count it gain whate'er befalleth.

3   O more and more thy love extend,
My life befriend with heav'nly pleasure;
That I may win thy paradise,
Thy pearl of price, thy countless treasure.
Since but in thee I can go free
From earthly care and vain oppression,
This prayer I make for Jesu's sake,
That thou me take in thy possession.

Robert Bridges (1844-1930)

The Congregation may prefer to sing from the Melody Version overleaf.

MELODY VERSION

CROSSINGS   C. ARMSTRONG GIBBS (1889–1960)

1 Thee will I love, my God and King, Thee will I
sing, my strength and tow - er: For ev - er -
more thee will I trust, O God most just of
truth and pow-er: Who all things hast in or - der
placed, Yea, for thy plea - sure hast cre - a -
ted; And on thy throne un - seen, un - known,
Reign-est a - lone in glo - ry seat - ed;

2 Set in my heart thy love I find; My wand'-ring
mind to thee thou lead-est; My trem-bling
hope, my strong de - sire, With heav'n-ly fire thou
kind - ly feed-est. Lo, all things fair thy path pre -
pare, Thy beau - ty to my spi - rit call -
eth, Thine to re - main in joy or pain,
And count it gain what - e'er be - fall - eth.

3 O more and more thy love ex - tend, My life be -
friend with heav'n - ly plea-sure; That I may
win thy pa - ra - dise, Thy pearl of price, thy
count-less trea-sure. Since but in thee I can go
free From earth-ly care and vain op - press -
ion, This prayer I make for Je - su's sake,
That thou me take in thy pos - sess - ion.

Robert Bridges (1844–1930)

66

GARELOCHSIDE S.M.   K. G. FINLAY (1882–   )

Unison

Alternative Tune, DAY OF PRAISE, M.H.B. 778

The Lord's Day

THE first day of the week,
His own, in sad despair,
Could not believe for very joy
The Risen Lord was there.

2 Now they obeyed his word,
Now shared what Jesus gave,
And, one in him, in breaking bread
Knew what it costs to save.

3 And each day of the week,
And on the Lord's own day,
They walked in Christian liberty
His new and living Way.

4 And on the Lord's own day,
From needless burdens freed,
They kept a Sabbath made for man,
To fit man's inmost need.

5 How soon men forge again
The fetters of their past!
As long as Jesus lives in us,
So long our freedoms last.

6 This day his people meet,
This day his word is sown.
Lord Jesus, show us how to use
This day we call your own.

F. Pratt Green (1903-   )

E

67

FIRST TUNE

ANDREW 66.66.88.
Unison

DAVID McCARTHY (1931–   )

1 The God who rules this earth gave life to ev-ery race; He chose its day of birth, the col-our of its face; So none may claim su - per-ior grade wi-thin the fa-mi - ly he's made.

Music: © David McCarthy.   Words: © Galliard Ltd.

SECOND TUNE

LAWES' PSALM 47 66.66.88.   Melody and bass by HENRY LAWES (1596–1662)
(rhythm slightly altered)

About Race and War

THE God who rules this earth
gave life to every race;
He chose its day of birth,
the colour of its face;
So none may claim superior grade
within the family he's made.

2
But sin infects us all,
distorts the common good;
The universal fall
corrupts all brotherhood;
So racial pride and colour strife
spread fear and hate throughout
    man's life.

3
Between the West and East,
yet neither black nor white,
Behold! God's Son released!
in whom all men unite.
He comes with unrestricted grace
to heal the hearts of every race.

4
That Man alone combines
all lives within his own:
That Man alone enshrines
all flesh, all blood, all bone;
That Man accepts all human pain,
that Man breaks death, that Man
    shall reign.

5.
To him we bring our praise,
on him all hopes depend;
Sole Master of our days,
in him we see the End;
Man's final Lord, God's perfect Son,
in Jesus Christ are all made one.

Richard G. Jones (1926-   )

68

REDEMPTOR S.M.

JOHN WILSON (1905–)

Unison

He is our Peace

T HE Saviour's precious blood
Hath made all nations one.
United let us praise this deed
The Father's love hath done.

2 In this vast world of men,
A world so full of sin,
No other theme can be our prayer
Than this—thy Kingdom come.

3 In this sad world of war
Can peace be ever found?
Unless the love of Christ prevail,
True peace will not abound.

4 The Master's new command
Was—love each other well.
O brothers, let us all unite
To do his holy will.

Tai Jun Park (Korea)
Tr. William Scott and Yung Oon Kim (1950)

69

GONFALON ROYAL L.M.

Unison. With movement.

P. C. BUCK (1871–1947)

A — — men.

The Institution of a Gospel Ministry from Christ

THE Saviour, when to heaven he rose,
In splendid triumph o'er his foes,
Scattered his gifts on men below,
And wide his royal bounties flow.

2 Hence sprung th' apostles' honoured name,
Sacred beyond heroic fame;
In lowlier forms, to bless our eyes,
Pastors from hence, and teachers rise.

3 From Christ their varied gifts derive,
And fed by Christ their graces live;
While, guarded by his mighty hand,
Midst all the rage of hell they stand.

4 So shall the bright succession run
Through the last courses of the sun;
While unborn churches by their care
Shall rise and flourish large and fair.

5 Jesus our Lord their hearts shall know—
The Spring whence all these blessings flow;
Pastors and people shout his praise
Through all the round of endless days. *Amen.*

Philip Doddridge† (1702–51)

Music: © Oxford University Press.

70

VRUECHTEN 67.67.D.   Dutch Melody, 17th century

Come, share our Eas - ter joy That death could not im - pri - son,

Nor an - y power des - troy, Our Christ, who is a - ri - sen, a -

ri - sen, a - ri - sen, a - ri - - - - sen!

Our Christ is Arisen

THIS joyful Eastertide
  What need is there for grieving?
Cast all your cares aside
  And be not unbelieving:

> Come, share our Easter joy
>   That death could not imprison,
> Nor any power destroy,
>   Our Christ, who is arisen!

2 No work for him is vain,
    No faith in him mistaken,
  For Easter makes it plain
    His Kingdom is not shaken:

3 Then put your trust in Christ,
    In waking or in sleeping.
  His grace on earth sufficed;
    He'll never quit his keeping:

F. Pratt Green (1903-   )

71

THORNBURY 76.76.D.

BASIL HARWOOD (1859–1949)

Unison (Vv. 1, 2 & 4). *Slow.*

The One People of God

THY hand, O God, has guided
  Thy flock, from age to age;
The wondrous tale is written,
  Full clear, on every page;
Our fathers owned thy goodness,
  And we their deeds record;
And both of this bear witness:
  One Church, one Faith, one Lord.

2 Thy heralds brought glad tidings
  To greatest, as to least;
They bade men rise, and hasten
  To share the great King's feast;
And this was all their teaching,
  In every deed and word,
To all alike proclaiming
  One Church, one Faith, one Lord.

3 Through many a day of darkness,
  Through many a scene of strife,
The faithful few fought bravely,
  To guard the nation's life.
Their Gospel of redemption,
  Sin pardoned, man restored,
Was all in this enfolded:
  One Church, one Faith, one Lord.

4 Thy mercy will not fail us,
  Nor leave thy work undone;
With thy right hand to help us,
  The vict'ry shall be won;
And then, by men and angels,
  Thy name shall be adored,
And this shall be their anthem:
  One Church, one Faith, one Lord.

E. H. Plumptre (1821-91)

See overleaf for Harmony version of Verse 3.

Verse 3. Harmony.

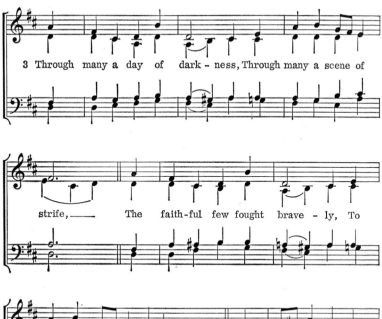

3 Through many a day of dark - ness, Through many a scene of

strife, —— The faith-ful few fought brave - ly, To

guard the na-tion's life.—— Their Gos - pel of re -

demp - tion, Sin par-doned, man re - stored, ——

One Church, one

Was all in this en - fold - ed: One Church, one

Organ

Faith, one Lord.

Faith, one Lord, one Faith, one Lord.

Turn back for Verse 4.

72

ENGELBERG 10 10 10.4.

Unison

C. V. STANFORD (1852–1924)

1 We know that Christ is raised and dies no more:

Embraced by fu-tile death he broke its hold: And man's des-

pair he turned to bla-zing joy: Al - le - lu - ia!

Verses 1-3

whole will sing:_____ Al - le - lu - ia! A - men.

Romans 6. 9

W E know that Christ is raised and dies no more:
Embraced by futile death he broke its hold:
And man's despair he turned to blazing joy:
Alleluia!

2 We share by water in his saving death:
This union brings to being one new cell,
A living and organic part of Christ:
Alleluia!

3 The Father's splendour clothes the Son with life:
The Spirit's fission shakes the Church of God:
Baptized we live with God the Three in One:
Alleluia!

4 A new Creation comes to life and grows
As Christ's new body takes on flesh and blood:
The universe restored and whole will sing:
Alleluia! *Amen.*

John B. Geyer (1932–   )

73

INTERCESSOR 11 10.11 10.   C. HUBERT H. PARRY (1848–1918)

The Family of Nations

W E turn to you, O God of every nation,
  Giver of Life and Origin of Good;
your love is at the heart of all creation,
  your hurt is people's broken brotherhood.

2 We turn to you, that we may be forgiven
  for crucifying Christ on earth again.
We know that we have never wholly striven,
  forgetting self, to love the other man.

3 Free every heart from pride and self-reliance,
  our ways of thought inspire with simple grace;
break down among us barriers of defiance,
  speak to the soul of all the human race.

4 Teach us, good Lord, to serve the need of others,
  help us to give and not to count the cost.
Unite us all for we are born as brothers;
  defeat our Babel with your Pentecost.

Fred Kaan (1929-   )

74

SUTTON TRINITY 65.65.D.

F. PRATT GREEN (1903–)

1 When the Church of Jesus
Shuts its out- er door,
Lest the roar of traf - fic
Drown the voice of prayer:
May our prayers, Lord, make us
Ten times more a - ware

That the world we ban-ish Is our Christian care.

The Church in the World

WHEN the Church of Jesus
  Shuts its outer door,
Lest the roar of traffic
  Drown the voice of prayer:
May our prayers, Lord, make us
  Ten times more aware
That the world we banish
  Is our Christian care.

2 If our hearts are lifted
    Where devotion soars
  High above this hungry
    Suffering world of ours:
  Lest our hymns should drug us
    To forget its needs,
  Forge our Christian worship
    Into Christian deeds.

3 Lest the gifts we offer,
    Money, talents, time,
  Serve to salve our conscience
    To our secret shame:
  Lord, reprove, inspire us
    By the way you give;
  Teach us, dying Saviour,
    How true Christians live.

F. Pratt Green (1903-   )

SONGS

75 Black is the Earth

Melody by BERNARD GREAVES (1936–
Harmonized by FRANCIS WESTBROOK (1903–

Unison. *Calm, not too slow*

1 Black is the earth and stark the trees, Brown the ri-ver, cool the breeze: But red is your blood and rich your life — Which we share in this sac-ri-fice.

(Vv. 2 & 5)

In other verses the words will dictate the details of the vocal rhythm.
Music and Words: © C. Vaughan.

(Not to be used with the accompaniment opposite)

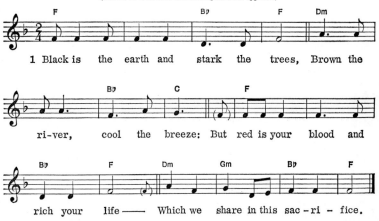

1 Black is the earth and stark the trees, Brown the ri-ver, cool the breeze: But red is your blood and rich your life —— Which we share in this sac-ri - fice.

Written in November, this song uses seasonal imagery to present by contrast the intimacy of Christ.

BLACK is the earth and stark the trees,
Brown the river, cool the breeze;
But red is your blood and rich your life—
Which we share in this sacrifice.

2 The moon is pale, the hills are far,
Horizons faint like the furthest star;
But Christ is close, his Kingdom near,
His voice is golden, strong and clear.

3 The fields are burnt, the corn long cut,
Flowers withered, windows shut;
But within our hearts, warm delight,
Brought by Christ our strength and light.

4 Take these gifts, though not ours to give,
Take these lives we badly live;
Accept them, marks of thankfulness,
Take them, raise them, change and bless.

5 We're citizens of a shattered world,
Where fists are clenched and lips are curled;
Through your power let bickering cease,
Through union in the Eucharist.

Christopher Vaughan (1942-   )

76

Mary's Child

('Born in the night')

Unison. Medium pace.

GEOFFREY AINGER (1925–)

1 Born— in the night, Ma-ry's Child, A long way from your home;— Com – ing in need, Ma-ry's Child, Born— in a bor-rowed room.

Mary's Child

BORN in the night,
Mary's Child,
A long way from your home:
Coming in need,
Mary's Child,
Born in a borrowed room.

2   Clear shining Light,
Mary's Child,
Your face lights up our way;
Light of the world,
Mary's Child,
Dawn on our darkened day.

3   Truth of our life,
Mary's Child,
You tell us God is good;
Prove it is true,
Mary's Child,
Go to your Cross of wood.

4   Hope of the world,
Mary's Child,
You're coming soon to reign;
King of the earth,
Mary's Child,
Walk in our streets again.

Geoffrey Ainger (1925-   )

77 Every Star shall sing a Carol

Unison. Gently, but not slow.

SYDNEY CARTER (1915–   )

1 Ev-ery star shall sing a car-ol; Ev-ery creature, high or low, Come and praise the King of Hea-ven By what-ev-er name you know: *God a-bove, Man be-low,*

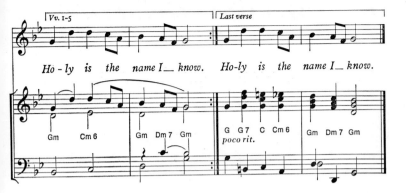

Ho-ly is the name I__ know. Ho-ly is the name I__ know.

Gm   Cm 6   Gm   Dm 7   Gm   G   G 7   C   Cm 6   Gm   Dm 7   Gm
                                  poco rit.

A Carol of the Universe

EVERY star shall sing a carol;
　　Every creature, high or low,
Come and praise the King of Heaven
　　By whatever name you know:

　　　God above, Man below,
　　　Holy is the name I know.

2 When the King of all creation
　　Had a cradle on the earth,
Holy was the human body,
　　Holy was the human birth:

3 Who can tell what other cradle,
　　High above the Milky Way,
Still may rock the King of Heaven
　　On another Christmas Day?

4 Who can count how many crosses,
　　Still to come or long ago,
Crucify the King of Heaven?
　　Holy is the name I know:

5 Who can tell what other body
　　He will hallow for his own?
I will praise the son of Mary,
　　Brother of my blood and bone:

6 Every star and every planet,
　　Every creature, high and low,
Come and praise the King of Heaven
　　By whatever name you know:

　　　　　　　Sydney Carter (1915-　　)

78 Fire is Lighting Torch and Lamp

FIRST TUNE

WESTHOLME

ERIC REID (1936–)

Pedal notes for an organ accompaniment are shown by downward stems.

now,　　Fill　all　our　lives　with　your　fire.＿＿＿　　light.

Creator Spirit

FIRE is lighting torch and lamp at night,
Fire outbursts into power and light.
　　Come, O God, Creator, Spirit, now,
　　Fill all our lives with your fire.

2 Wind is battering waves of sea on land;
　Wind is grinding the rocks to sand.
　　Come, O God, Creator, Spirit, now,
　　Order anew all your world.

3 Water gushes down the cleft of space,
　Living water and spring of grace.
　　Come, O God, Creator, Spirit, now,
　　Grant us your life and your light.

John B. Geyer (1932-　　)

Music: © *Galliard Ltd.*　　*Words:* © *J. B. Geyer.*

Fire is Lighting Torch and Lamp
SECOND TUNE

PETER
Unison

DAVID McCARTHY (1931–   )

1 Fire is light-ing torch and lamp at night,   Fire out-bursts in-to power and light.

Come, O God,   Cre-a-tor, Spi-rit, now,   Fill all our lives with your   fire.

Creator Spirit

FIRE is lighting torch and lamp at night,
Fire outbursts into power and light.
   Come, O God, Creator, Spirit, now,
   Fill all our lives with your fire.

2 Wind is battering waves of sea on land;
Wind is grinding the rocks to sand.
   Come, O God, Creator, Spirit, now,
   Order anew all your world.

3 Water gushes down the cleft of space,
Living water and spring of grace.
   Come, O God, Creator, Spirit, now,
   Grant us your life and your light.

John B. Geyer (1932–   )

79   God Holds the Key

GOD HOLDS THE KEY

G. C. STEBBINS (1846–1945)
(harmony revised)

1 God holds the key of all un-known, And I am glad;—
If o – ther hands should hold the key, Or if he trust – ed
it to me, I might be sad,— I might be sad.—

'Cast all your cares on him, for he cares about you'

GOD holds the key of all unknown,
  And I am glad;
If other hands should hold the key,
Or if he trusted it to me,
  I might be sad.

2 What if tomorrow's cares were here
  Without its rest!
I'd rather he unlocked the day;
And as the hours swing open, say,
  'Thy will is best'.

3 I cannot read his future plans,
  But this I know:
I have the smiling of his face,
And all the refuge of his grace,
  While here below.

4 Enough; this covers all my wants,
  And so I rest!
For what I cannot, he can see,
And in his care I saved shall be,
  For ever blest.

J. Parker (1830–1902)

80 God is Our Defence

Unison. About ♩=108

HEINZ W. ZIMMERMANN (1930–)

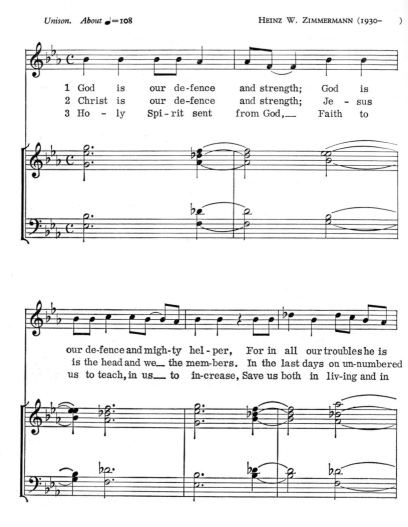

1 God is our de-fence and strength; God is
2 Christ is our de-fence and strength; Je - sus
3 Ho - ly Spi - rit sent from God,— Faith to

our de-fence and migh-ty hel - per, For in all our troubles he is
is the head and we— the mem-bers. In the last days on un-numbered
us to teach, in us— to in-crease, Save us both in liv-ing and in

REFRAIN

by us No matter what___ be-tide us:
plan-ets He will be hailed__'Im-man-uel':
dy - ing Thy tes-ta-ment___ im-bi-bing:

The Lord God of Hosts is

with us, The Lord God of Hosts,___ Ja-cob's God, Is___ our strong de-fence.

From the German of H. W. Zimmermann (1930-   )
based on Psalm 46
Tr. I. H. Jones (1934-   )

NOTE—*The verses may be sung by the Choir alone, the Congregation singing only the Refrain. Verse 1 may be sung by Tenors and Basses (with the accompaniment played an octave lower), Verse 2 by Sopranos and Altos, and Verse 3 by Full Choir.*

Music and Words: © Bärenreiter & Co.

81   I Come Ever Singing

Moving freely   THE EVANGELICAL SISTERS OF MARY (DARMSTADT) (1955)   Melody by

1 I come ev-er sing-ing, The ve-ry air___ ring-ing,

'Our Fa-ther in hea-ven is lov-ing—all love!

His heart's full of kind-ness, A heart of love___ on - ly,

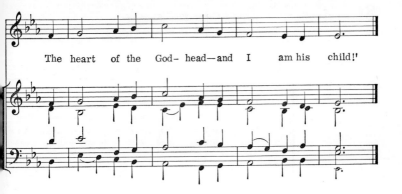

The heart of the God-head—and I am his child!'

'Sing psalms and hymns and spiritual songs with
gratitude in your hearts to God'.

I COME ever singing,
The very air ringing,
'Our Father in heaven is loving—all love!
His heart's full of kindness,
A heart of love only,
The heart of the Godhead—and I am his child!'

2 I come with my praises
For love which so amazes
The hearts of his children, once full of their sin:
'His heart's full of kindness,
A heart of love only,
The heart of the Godhead—our Father is he!'

3 I come all rejoicing,
Creation's joy voicing,
'Our Father in heaven is loving—all love!
His heart's full of kindness,
A heart of love only,
The heart of the Godhead—our Father is he!'

4 I praise him with yearning,
That all the world turning
In love to the heart of their Father above
May joyfully witness
That God indeed is Father,
And praise him because he is loving—all love!

The Evangelical Sisters of Mary (Darmstadt)† (1955)

I Come Ever Singing
VERSION FOR WOMEN'S VOICES

MELODY

1 I come ev - er sing - ing, The
2 I come with my prai - ses For
3 I come all re - joic - ing, Cre -
4 I praise him with yearn - ing, That

ACCOMPANYING VOICES

ve - ry air___ ring - ing, 'Our Fa - ther in
love which so a - ma - zes The hearts of his
a - tion's joy___ voic - ing, 'Our Fa - ther in
all the world___ turn - ing In love to the

hea - ven is lov - ing— all love! His
chil - dren, once full of their sin: 'His
hea - ven is lov - ing— all love! His
heart of their Fa - ther a - bove May

heart's full of kind - ness, A heart of love___ on - ly,
heart's full of kind - ness, A heart of love___ on - ly,
heart's full of kind - ness, A heart of love___ on - ly,
joy - ful - ly wit - ness That God in - deed is Fa - ther,

The heart of the God - head—and I am his Child!'
The heart of the God - head—our Fa - ther is he!'
The heart of the God - head—our Fa - ther is he!'
And praise him be - cause he is lov - ing—all love!

Words† and Music by
The Evangelical Sisters of Mary (Darmstadt) (1955)

Music and Words: © The Evangelical Sisters of Mary (Darmstadt)

82 Lord of the Dance

('I danced in the morning')

This modern ballad continues the tradition of the English carol 'Tomorrow shall be my Dancing Day', in which the Son of God says that the purpose of his incarnation is 'to call my true love (i.e. mankind) to my dances'. The image conveys the love and joy of Christian life and is thoroughly compatible with Scripture.

Lively and rhythmic
Unison (or Solo)

Adapted from a traditional melody, by SYDNEY CARTER (1915–   )
(Organ accompaniment by A. G. MATHEW)

Music and Words: © 1963 Sydney Carter © 1968, 1969 Galliard Ltd.

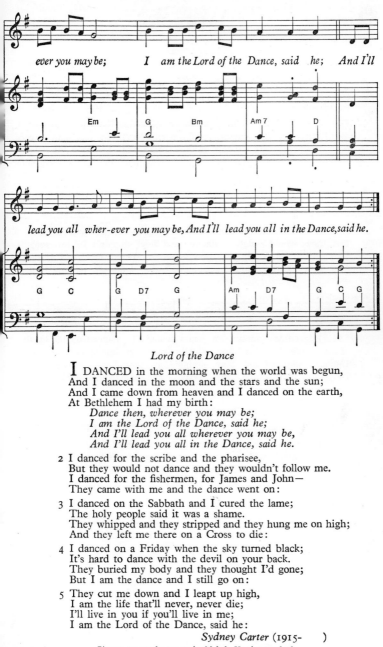

ever you may be; I am the Lord of the Dance, said he; And I'll

lead you all wher-ever you may be, And I'll lead you all in the Dance, said he.

Lord of the Dance

I DANCED in the morning when the world was begun,
And I danced in the moon and the stars and the sun;
And I came down from heaven and I danced on the earth,
At Bethlehem I had my birth:
>   *Dance then, wherever you may be;*
>   *I am the Lord of the Dance, said he;*
>   *And I'll lead you all wherever you may be,*
>   *And I'll lead you all in the Dance, said he.*

2 I danced for the scribe and the pharisee,
But they would not dance and they wouldn't follow me.
I danced for the fishermen, for James and John—
They came with me and the dance went on:

3 I danced on the Sabbath and I cured the lame;
The holy people said it was a shame.
They whipped and they stripped and they hung me on high;
And they left me there on a Cross to die:

4 I danced on a Friday when the sky turned black;
It's hard to dance with the devil on your back.
They buried my body and they thought I'd gone;
But I am the dance and I still go on:

5 They cut me down and I leapt up high,
I am the life that'll never, never die;
I'll live in you if you'll live in me;
I am the Lord of the Dance, said he:

Sydney Carter (1915-   )

Singers may prefer to use the Melody Version overleaf.

Lord of the Dance
('I danced in the morning')

MELODY VERSION

Lively and rhythmic

Adapted from a traditional melody
by SYDNEY CARTER (1915–   )

Unison voices (or Solo)

1 I danced in the morn-ing when the world was be-gun,
2 I danced for the scribe and the pha - ri - see,
3 I danced on the Sabbath and I cured the lame;
4 I danced on a Friday when the sky turned black;

And I danced in the moon and the stars_ and the sun;
But they would not dance and they wouldn't fol-low me.
The_ ho - ly_ peo - ple_ said it was a shame.
It's_ hard to_ dance with the de-vil on your back.

And I came down from hea-ven and I danced on the earth,
I_ danced for the fisher - men, for James and_ John;
They_ whipped and they stripp'd and they hung me on high;
They_ bur - ied my body_ and they thought I'd_ gone;

At Beth - le - hem I_ had my birth:
They came with_ me and the dance went on:
And they left me_ there on a Cross to die:
But I am the dance and I still go on:

REFRAIN

Dance then, wher - ever you may be; I am the Lord of the Dance, said he; And I'll

lead you all, wher - ever you may be, And I'll lead you all in the Dance, said he.

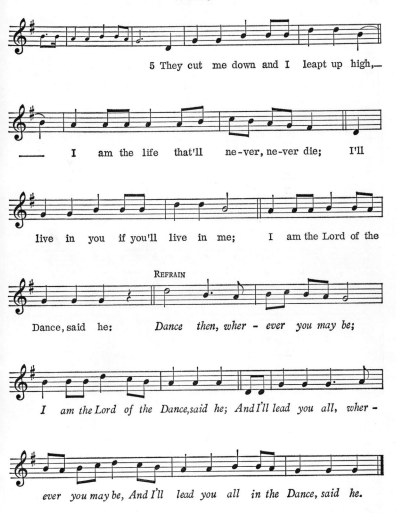

5 They cut me down and I leapt up high,—
— I am the life that'll ne-ver, ne-ver die; I'll
live in you if you'll live in me; I am the Lord of the

REFRAIN

Dance, said he: *Dance then, wher - ever you may be;*
I am the Lord of the Dance, said he; And I'll lead you all, wher -
ever you may be, And I'll lead you all in the Dance, said he.

Sydney Carter (1915-   )

83 Jesus the Lord said

YISU NE KAHA

Unison

Urdu melody
Harmonized by FRANCIS WESTBROOK (1903-)

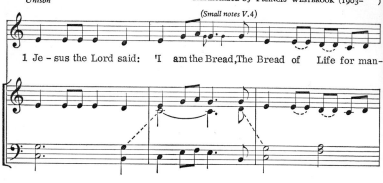

1 Je – sus the Lord said: 'I am the Bread, The Bread of Life for man-

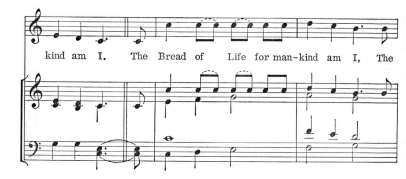

kind am I. The Bread of Life for man-kind am I, The

Bread of Life for man – kind am I'. Je – sus the Lord said:

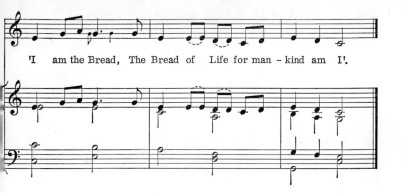

'I am the Bread, The Bread of Life for man – kind am I'.

The Voice of Jesus

JESUS the Lord said: 'I am the Bread,
The Bread of Life for mankind am I.
    The Bread of Life for mankind am I,
    The Bread of Life for mankind am I'.
Jesus the Lord said: 'I am the Bread,
The Bread of Life for mankind am I'.

2 Jesus the Lord said: 'I am the Door,
The Way and the Door for the poor am I'.

3 Jesus the Lord said: 'I am the Light,
The one true Light of the world am I'.

4 Jesus the Lord said: 'I am the Shepherd,
The one Good Shepherd of the sheep am I'.

5 Jesus the Lord said: 'I am the Life,
The Resurrection and the Life am I'.

Anonymous
Tr. from the Urdu by Dermott Monahan (1906-57)

Music: © The Methodist Youth Department

84   Let us Break Bread Together

Negro Spiritual,
arranged by CHARLES CLEALL (1927–)

1 Let us break bread to-ge-ther on our knees; Let us break bread to-ge-ther on our knees:

REFRAIN

When I fall on my knees, With my face to the ri-sing sun, O Lord, have mer-cy on me.

Let us break bread together . . .

LET us break bread together on our knees;
Let us break bread together on our knees:

When I fall on my knees,
With my face to the rising sun,
O Lord, have mercy on me.

2 Let us drink wine together on our knees;
Let us drink wine together on our knees:

3 Let us praise God together on our knees;
Let us praise God together on our knees:

Negro Spiritual

OPTIONAL CHORAL ACCOMPANIMENT FOR VERSE 3

Sopranos sing words of V.3.   A.T.B. sing vowel 'Oo' or 'Ah'
Organ plays accompaniment on facing page

(S.A.T.B.)
When I fall on my knees, With my
face to the ri-sing sun, O Lord, have mer-cy on me.

85 Dialogue

('Life has many Rhythms')

JONATHAN 65.65.D.

ROBIN SHELDON (1932–)

Unison

1 Life has ma-ny rhy-thms, ev - ery heart its beat;—

Ev - ery-where we hear the sound of danc-ing feet.

Life is this world's sec-ret: Lord — of Life, for - give,—

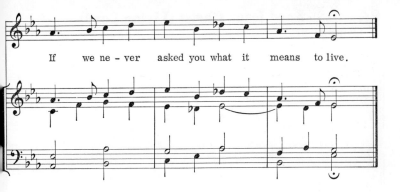

If we ne-ver asked you what it means to live.

Dialogue

LIFE has many rhythms, every heart its beat;
Everywhere we hear the sound of dancing feet.
Life is this world's secret: Lord of Life, forgive,
If we never asked you what it means to live.

2 *Life is meant for loving*. Lord, if this is true,
Why do millions suffer without help from you?
Some who fought injustice added wrong to wrong:
Can it be that love is stronger than the strong?

3 It was you who promised: *All who seek shall find.*
What we find lies deeper than our reach of mind;
What we found was you, Lord, you the God Above,
You had come, as Victim, to the world you love!

4 *Life is meant for loving*. Lord, if this is true,
Love of life and neighbour spring from love of you.
Give us your compassion: yours the name we bear;
Yours the only victory we would serve and share.

F. Pratt Green (1903-   )

Music: © Robin Sheldon.   Words: © Oxford University Press

86   Lord Jesus Christ (Living Lord)

LIVING LORD
Slow Beat Ballad

PATRICK APPLEFORD (1925-)

1 Lord Je-sus Christ, You___ have come to us, You___ are one with us, Ma—ry's Son. Clean-sing our souls from all their sin, Pour-ing your love and good-ness in, Je-sus, our love for

you we sing, Liv-ing Lord.

A Communion Prayer

LORD Jesus Christ,
You have come to us,
You are one with us,
    Mary's Son.
Cleansing our souls from all their sin,
Pouring your love and goodness in,
Jesus, our love for you we sing,
    Living Lord.

2   Lord Jesus Christ,
    Now and every day
    Teach us how to pray
        Son of God.
You have commanded us to do
This, in remembrance, Lord, of you:
Into our lives your power breaks through,
        Living Lord.

3   Lord Jesus Christ,
    You have come to us,
    Born as one of us,
        Mary's Son.
Led out to die on Calvary,
Risen from death to set us free,
Living Lord Jesus, help us see
        You are Lord.

4   Lord Jesus Christ,
    I would come to you,
    Live my life for you,
        Son of God.
All your commands I know are true,
Your many gifts will make me new,
Into my life your power breaks through,
        Living Lord.

Patrick Appleford (1925-   )

Music and Words : © *J. Weinberger Ltd*

87   Lord, look upon our working days

ST BLANE

ERIK ROUTLEY (1917–   )

Unison. Slowly

1 Lord, look up-on our work-ing days, Bu-sied in fac-tory, of - fice, store; May word-less work thy name a - dore, The

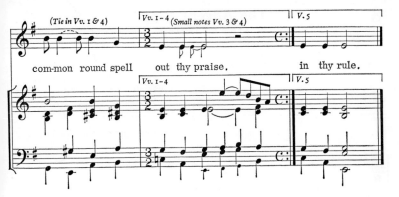

com-mon round spell   out thy praise.   in thy rule.

NOTE—*This hymn and its tune are perhaps best suited to a service of a special character incorporating some form of drama. The hymn should be sung without pauses between the verses, but the interlude may be varied at the accompanist's discretion provided that the number of beats in the last bar remain constant.*

Christ the Workman

LORD, look upon our working days,
Busied in factory, office, store;
May wordless work thy name adore,
The common round spell out thy praise?

2 Bent to the lot our crafts assign,
Swayed by deep tides of need and fear,
In loyalties torn, the truth unclear,
How may we build to thy design?

3 Thou art the workman, Lord, not we:
All worlds were made at thy command.
Christ, their sustainer, bared his hand,
Rescued them from futility.

4 Our part to do what he'll commit,
Who strides the world, and calls men all
Partners in pain and carnival,
To grasp the hope he won for it.

5 Cover our faults with pardon full,
Shield those who suffer when we shirk:
Take what is worthy in our work,
Give it its portion in thy rule.

Ian Fraser (1917-   )

Music: © *Galliard Ltd.   Words:* © *Ian Fraser*

88

The Advent Ring
('One red candle')

On each Sunday in Advent, verses of this song may be sung while the candles for the day are lit on the Advent Ring—recalling the witnesses to the coming of the True Light.

A. R. FRANKLIN (1954–)
Accompaniment by M. DORNAY and I. H. JONES

1 One red can-dle, burn-ing bright, burn-ing bright, burn-ing bright; Pro-phets shining through the night, through the night.

The Advent Ring

ONE red candle, burning bright;
Prophets shining through the night.

2 John the Baptist, straight and strong,
Points the way to go along.

3 Mother Mary now we bless.
God had called. She answered, 'Yes'.

4 We are waiting, Lord, for you.
We're a shining candle too.

5 Born a baby in a stall,
Jesus, brightest light of all.

Emily Chisholm (1910–)

ADDITIONAL INSTRUMENTAL ACCOMPANIMENT

(1) *Voices and Treble Instruments, Glockenspiel, etc.*
(2) *Organ or Piano*
(3) *Three Recorders, or other Wind Instruments, or Muted Violins*
(4) *Guitars*
(5) *Any plucked Instrument. (Chime or Cymbal may be added)*

This Song may be sung using (1) and (2) alone, or with suitable additions of (3), (4) and (5).

89   Our Father

West Indian Calypso
Arranged O. G. BLARR (1934–   )

1 Our____ Fa - ther, who art in hea - ven,
2 On the earth as it is in ____ hea - ven,
3 And for - give us all our____ trespasses,
4 Lead us not in - to temp - ta - tion,
5 Thine is the King-dom, the pow'r and the glo - ry,

Hallowed be thy

Name!

1 Thy King-dom come, thy will be__ done,__
2 Give us this day__ our dai - ly__ bread,__
3 As we forgive those who tres-pass a-gainst us,
4 But de - li - ver us__ from all that is e - vil,
5 For ev - er and ev-er, for ev - er and ev - er,

*If preferred, the Congregation may sing only the Refrain 'Hallowed be thy Name!'

Hal-lowed be thy Name! A - men.

The following solo for Wind Instrument may be played before Vv. 1 and 5, with accompaniment as for a normal complete verse.

(small notes if clarinet is used)

90 Peter feared the Cross

CONFESSION

FRANCIS WESTBROOK (1903-)

1 Pe-ter feared the Cross for him - self and his Mas-ter; Pe-ter temp-ted Je-sus to turn and go back. O Lord, have mer-cy, Ligh-ten our dark-ness. We've all been temp-ters, Our light is black.

Peter feared the Cross

PETER feared the Cross for himself and his Master;
Peter tempted Jesus to turn and go back.
 O Lord, have mercy,
 Lighten our darkness.
 We've all been tempters,
 Our light is black.

2 Judas loved his pride and rejected his Master;
Judas turned a traitor and lost his way back.
 O Lord, have mercy,
 Lighten our darkness.
 We've all been traitors,
 Our light is black.

3 Peter, James and John fell asleep when their Master
asked them to be praying a few paces back.
 O Lord, have mercy,
 Lighten our darkness.
 We've all been sleeping,
 Our light is black.

4 Peter, vexed and tired, thrice denied his own Master;
Said he never knew him, to stop a girl's clack.
 O Lord, have mercy,
 Lighten our darkness.
 We've all denied you,
 Our light is black.

5 Twelve all ran away and forsook their dear Master;
Left him, lonely prisoner, a lamb in wolves' pack.
 O Lord, have mercy,
 Lighten our darkness,
 We've all been failures,
 Our light is black.

6 Pilate asked the crowd to set free their good Master.
'Crucify', they shouted, 'we don't want him back!'
 O Lord, have mercy,
 Lighten our darkness.
 We crucified you,
 Our light is black.

7 We have watched the Cross and we've scoffed at the Master;
Thought the safe way better and tried our own tack.
 O Lord, have mercy,
 Lighten our darkness.
 We've all reviled you,
 Our light is black.

Emily Chisholm (1910-)

(For a shorter version of this song, verses 2, 3 and 6 may be omitted.)

91 Judas and Mary
('Said Judas to Mary')

This song explores the meaning for today of the story recorded in St John, chapter 12, verses 1-8.

SYDNEY CARTER (1915–)
(accompaniment adapted)

Unison. Very smoothly and gently.

1 Said Ju-das to Ma-ry,'Now what will you do With your oint-ment so rich and so rare?' 'I'll pour it all ov-er the feet of the Lord,And I'll wipe it a-way with my

hair', she said, 'I'll wipe it a - way with my hair'.____

C D Bm Em Am Bm Em

Judas and Mary

SAID Judas to Mary, 'Now what will you do
  With your ointment so rich and so rare?'
'I'll pour it all over the feet of the Lord,
And I'll wipe it away with my hair', she said,
  'I'll wipe it away with my hair'.

2 'Oh Mary, Oh Mary, Oh think of the poor—
  This ointment, it could have been sold;
And think of the blankets and think of the bread
You could buy with the silver and gold', he said,
  'You could buy with the silver and gold'.

3 'Tomorrow, tomorrow I'll think of the poor,
  Tomorrow', she said, 'not today;
For dearer than all of the poor in the world
Is my love who is going away', she said,
  'My love who is going away'.

4 Said Jesus to Mary, 'Your love is so deep,
  Today you may do as you will;
Tomorrow, you say, I am going away,
But my body I leave with you still', he said,
  'My body I leave with you still'.

5 'The poor of the world are my body', he said,
  'To the end of the world they shall be;
The bread and the blankets you give to the poor
You'll find you have given to me', he said,
  'You'll find you have given to me'.

6 'My body will hang on the cross of the world
  Tomorrow', he said, 'and today,
And Martha and Mary will find me again
And wash all my sorrow away', he said,
  'And wash all my sorrow away'.

Sydney Carter (1915-)

92 Trotting, Trotting through Jerusalem

ERIC REID (1936–)

Unison

1 Trot-ting, trot-ting through Je – ru – sa – lem, Je-sus, sit-ting on a— don – key's back, chil-dren wav-ing bran-ches, sing-ing 'Hap-py is he that comes in the name of the

Pedal notes for an organ accompaniment are shown by downward stems.

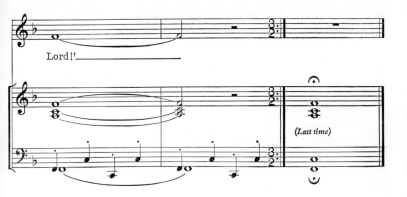

Lord!'

Palm Sunday

TROTTING, trotting through Jerusalem,
Jesus, sitting on a donkey's back,
children waving branches, singing
'Happy is he that comes in the name of the Lord!'

2   Many people in Jerusalem
    thought he should have come on a mighty horse
    leading all the Jews to battle—
    'Happy is he that comes in the name of the Lord!'

3   Many people in Jerusalem
    were amazed to see such a quiet man
    trotting, trotting on a donkey—
    'Happy is he that comes in the name of the Lord!'

4   Trotting, trotting through Jerusalem,
    Jesus, sitting on a donkey's back:
    Let us join the children singing
    'Happy is he that comes in the name of the Lord!'

Eric Reid (1936-   )

Music and Words: © Galliard Ltd.

93

Were You There?

Negro Spiritual
Arranged by Francis Westbrook (1903–)

Melody

Harmony (Sopranos sing words above)

1 Were you there when they cru-ci-fied my Lord?
2 Were you there when they nailed him to the tree?
3 Were you there when they laid him in the tomb?

1 Were you there when they cru-ci-fied my Lord, were you there?
2 Were you there when they nailed him to the tree, were you there?
3 Were you there when they laid him in the tomb, were you there?

Were you there when they cru-ci-fied my Lord?
Were you there when they nailed him to the tree?
Were you there when they laid him in the tomb?

Were you there when they cru-ci-fied my Lord, when they
Were you there when they nailed him to the tree, when they
Were you there when they laid him in the tomb, when they

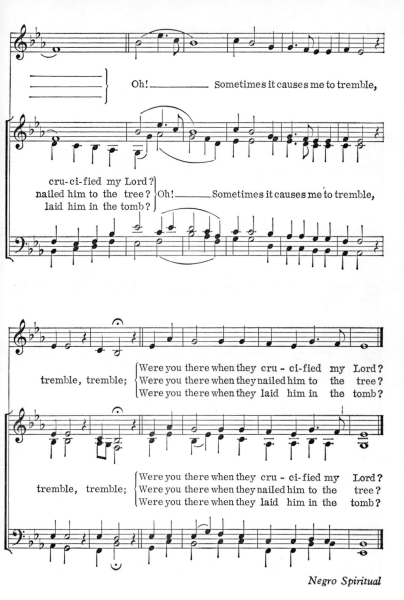

Oh!_____ Sometimes it causes me to tremble,

cru-ci-fied my Lord?
nailed him to the tree? }Oh!_____Sometimes it causes me to tremble,
laid him in the tomb?

tremble, tremble; {Were you there when they cru - ci-fied my Lord?
Were you there when they nailed him to the tree?
Were you there when they laid him in the tomb?

tremble, tremble; {Were you there when they cru - ci-fied my Lord?
Were you there when they nailed him to the tree?
Were you there when they laid him in the tomb?

Negro Spiritual

(It may be desirable to sing this tune a semitone higher.)

94   What Wondrous Love

Melody from *Southern Harmony* (1835)
Harmonized by C. R. Young (1926–   )

Unison.   *Rather slowly*

1 What won-drous love is this, O my soul, O my soul, What

won-drous love is this, O my soul! What won-drous love is this That

caused the Lord of bliss To lay a-side his crown for my

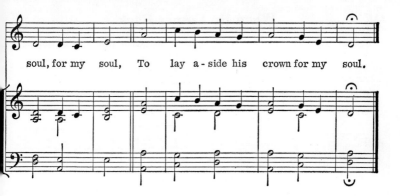

soul, for my soul, To lay a-side his crown for my soul.

The Eternal Theme

WHAT wondrous love is this, O my soul, O my soul,
What wondrous love is this, O my soul!
What wondrous love is this
That caused the Lord of bliss
To lay aside his crown for my soul, for my soul,
To lay aside his crown for my soul.

2 To God and to the Lamb I will sing, I will sing,
To God and to the Lamb I will sing;
To God and to the Lamb
Who is the great I AM,
While millions join the theme, I will sing, I will sing,
While millions join the theme, I will sing.

3 And when from death I'm free I'll sing on, I'll sing on,
And when from death I'm free I'll sing on.
And when from death I'm free
I'll sing and joyful be,
And through eternity I'll sing on, I'll sing on,
And through eternity I'll sing on.

American Folk Hymn

95

When He Comes Back

MALCOLM STEWART (1925–)
Arranged by IVOR H. JONES (1934–)

When he comes back, when he comes back, Our lamps will be burning to welcome him when he comes back.

*After last Refrain
go to 𝄋*

VERSES

1 The Mas-ter has prom-ised that he will re-turn On a
2 Look not for the Mas-ter in hea-ven's dark space; By the
3 This stran-ger will search for his home in the night, And then

night when there's no one ex - pect-ing   to   see him at   all._____
light of our   liv - ing on earth we'll dis - cov - er his   face._____
how will he   find it un - less all the win - dows are   bright?_____

Keep oil in the lamps so they're   rea - dy to   burn On the
The   face of the Mas - ter   is   al - ways at   hand In the
But   if   we are wai - ting—why   then he'll come in, And there'll

night of   his   sec - ret, when those who are   wait - ing he'll   call._____
face   of   the   stran-ger, the   poor in the   face of a   man._____
be   a   home com-ing with danc-ing and   sing - ing with   in._____

Back to REFRAIN 𝄋 *After last* REFRAIN

Malcolm Stewart (1925-   )

G

He Will Hold Me Fast

('When I fear my faith will fail')

HE WILL HOLD ME FAST

ROBERT HARKNESS (1880–1961)
(harmony slightly altered)

1 When I fear my faith will fail— Christ will hold me fast;

When the tempter would pre-vail— He can hold me fast:—

REFRAIN

He will hold me fast,—— He will hold me fast;

He will hold me, hold me fast, He will hold me, hold me fast,

He will hold me fast,—— He will hold me fast,——

For my Sa-viour loves me so,— He will hold me fast.

He will hold me fast

WHEN I fear my faith will fail
Christ will hold me fast;
When the tempter would prevail
He can hold me fast:

He will hold me fast,
He will hold me fast;
For my Saviour loves me so,
He will hold me fast.

2 I could never keep my hold,
He must hold me fast;
For my love is often cold,
He must hold me fast:

3 I am precious in his sight,
He will hold me fast;
Those he saves are his delight
He will hold me fast:

4 He'll not let my soul be lost,
Christ will hold me fast;
Bought by him at such a cost,
He will hold me fast:

Ada R. Habershon (1861-1918)

97   When I Needed a Neighbour

Melody by SYDNEY CARTER (1915–
Arranged by M. DORNAY and I. H. JONE

1 When I need-ed a neighbour, were you there, were you there?

When I need-ed a neighbour, were you there?   *And the*

This song may be accompanied by guitars alone, or by organ alone, or by guitars and organ together.

Music and Words: © 1965 Sydney Carter   © 1968, 1969 Galliard Ltd.

(v.7. *I'll be there.*)

creed and the col-our and the   name won't mat-ter, Were you there?

The Final Judgment?

WHEN I needed a neighbour, were you there, were you there?
When I needed a neighbour, were you there?
And the creed and the colour and the name won't matter,
Were you there?

2 I was hungry and thirsty, were you there, were you there?
I was hungry and thirsty, were you there?

3 I was cold, I was naked, were you there, were you there?
I was cold, I was naked, were you there?

4 When I needed a shelter, were you there, were you there?
When I needed a shelter, were you there?

5 When I needed a healer, were you there, were you there?
When I needed a healer, were you there?

6 When they put me in prison, were you there, were you there?
When they put me in prison, were you there?

7 Wherever you travel, I'll be there, I'll be there,
Wherever you travel, I'll be there.

And the creed and the colour and the name won't matter,
I'll be there.

Sydney Carter (1915-   )

98 In Honour of Saint Andrew
('When Jesus walked by Galilee')

STAWARD PEEL 88.66.

ERIK ROUTLEY (1917–

1 When Je - sus walked by Ga - li - lee, And cried to An - drew, 'Fol - low me!', He dropt his nets and went.—— Would I were such a saint!——

Music © Erik Routley   Words: © Oxford University Press

In Honour of Saint Andrew

WHEN Jesus walked by Galilee,
And cried to Andrew, 'Follow me!',
    He dropt his nets and went.
    Would I were such a saint!

2 Though some were favoured more than he,
And he was fourth and they 'the three',
    Yet Andrew was content.
    Would I were such a saint!

3 Of him they said, both Jew and Greek:
'Ask Andrew, if it's Christ you seek'.
    He knew why they were sent.
    Would I were such a saint!

4 So, far and wide, the legends prove
Here Andrew lived and here his love
    Had taught men to repent.
    Would I were such a saint!

5 Saint Andrew, wear a martyr's crown!
You were, in life and death, his own;
    For him your life was spent.
    Would I were such a saint!

F. Pratt Green (1903-   )

99 Christ In Need

('You needed a stable')

THURNE
Unison

IDA PRINS-BUTTLE (1908–   )

1 You need-ed a sta - ble the night you were born,__ A man-ger to serve as your bed,__ You need-ed a girl__ from a coun-try town And a light__ where the cat - tle

2 You need-ed a school - boy to give you his lunch,__ A lit - tle to feed a great crowd,__ You need-ed the fish__ and the home-made bread And you asked__ for the help__ of

3 You need-ed a don - key to ride in - to town,__ A friend's room for sup - per that night,__ You need-ed a band__ of__ com - mon men And their songs__ in the eve - ning

4 You need-ed a stran - ger to help with your cross,__ A Si - mon to car - ry your load,__ You need-ed his back__ in the jeers and shouts And the whips__ on the nar - row

fed;   Then as you grew___   In wis-dom and strength___ And
God;   As you drew near___   To **pas-sion** and death___ And
light;   Out in the dark___ While kneel-ing in prayer___ In
road;   But for his strength_ You would-n't have been___

came___ to know_ your God,___ You need-ed a   join - er's
thought_ of **tri-al** and cross,_ You need-ed a   street-girl's
grim ___ Geth-se – **ma** – ne,___ You need-ed to   have watch
Hois – ted up___ on high ___ And we wouldn't have   seen your

work- shop___ Be-side___ a   vil – lage   road.___
oint - ment___ To sig – ni – fy___ your   loss.___
with you___ Your friends from   Ga – li – lee.___
glo – – – ry un-der the   low' – ring   sky.___

Geoffrey Ainger (1925-   )

Music: © Mrs. Ida Prins-Buttle   Words: © Geoffrey Ainger

NOTE

Numbers *100*, *101* and *102* are examples of the type of psalmody introduced by Father Joseph Gelineau.

The canticles and psalms, in new translations, are sung to simple musical phrases with a steady semibreve 'beat'. Speech-rhythm is used as far as possible, provided that the main verbal stresses (shown in bold type) occur regularly. Unstressed syllables at the start of a phrase are sung as an 'up-beat', using the blackened note. When there are no such syllables, the preparatory bar remains in the accompaniment.

A feature of the psalmody is the optional use of an 'Antiphon' or refrain, to precede or follow individual verses or groups of verses. In the Te Deum (No. *100*) the antiphons are allocated to the choir. In other cases the same procedure may be adopted, introducing antiphons as often as desired. Alternatively, if the choir sings the verses of the psalm, the congregation may sing an antiphon as a refrain.

It is important to preserve an unbroken 'beat' through verses and antiphons alike. The unit-note representing one beat in the antiphon may differ from the standard semibreve-unit in the verses, but there should be no interruption of pulse at the transition.

(The setting of Psalm 23 has some musical features that are not found in normal Gelineau psalmody).

CANTICLES and PSALMS

100

Te Deum

('You we praise as God')

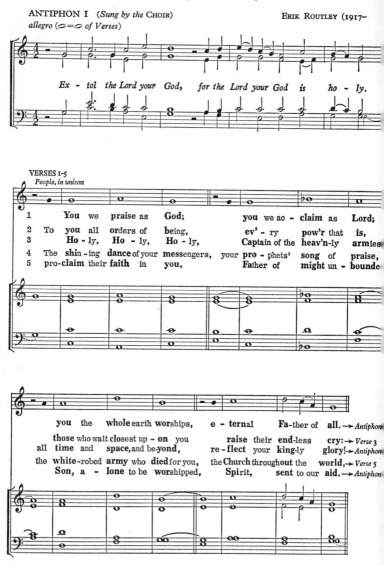

ANTIPHON I (*Sung by the* CHOIR)

ERIK ROUTLEY (1917–

allegro (♩=♩ *of Verses*)

Ex - tol the Lord your God, for the Lord your God is ho - ly.

VERSES 1-5
People, in unison

1 You we praise as God; you we ac - claim as Lord;
2 To you all orders of being, ev' - ry pow'r that is,
3 Ho - ly, Ho - ly, Ho - ly, Captain of the heav'n-ly armies
4 The shin - ing dance of your messengers, your pro - phets' song of praise,
5 pro-claim their faith in you, Father of might un - bounde

you the whole earth worships, e - ternal Fa-ther of all. → *Antiphon*
those who wait closest up - on you raise their end-less cry: → *Verse 3*
all time and space, and be-yond, re - flect your king-ly glory! → *Antiphon*
the white-robed army who died for you, the Church throughout the world, → *Verse 5*
Son, a - lone to be worshipped, Spirit, sent to our aid. → *Antiphon*

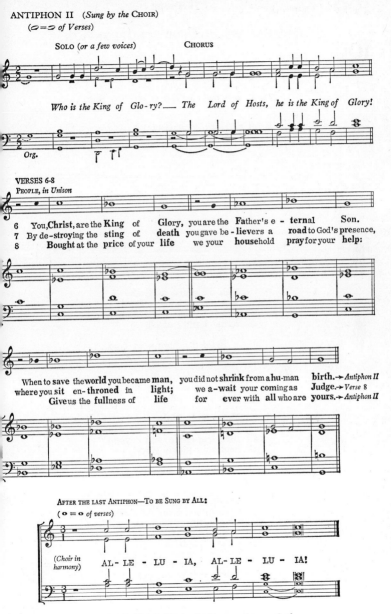

ANTIPHON II (*Sung by the* CHOIR)
(○ = ○ *of Verses*)

SOLO (*or a few voices*)   CHORUS

Who is the King of Glo-ry? ___ The Lord of Hosts, he is the King of Glory!

Org.

VERSES 6-8
PEOPLE, *in Unison*

6   You, **Christ**, are the **King** of   **Glory**, you are the **Father's** e - **ternal**   **Son.**
7   By de-**stroying** the **sting** of   **death** you gave be - **lievers** a   **road** to God's presence,
8   **Bought** at the **price** of your **life**   we your **household**   **pray** for your **help:**

When to save the **world** you became **man**, you did not **shrink** from a hu-man   **birth.** ⟶ *Antiphon II*
where you sit en-**throned** in   **light;**   we a-**wait** your coming as   **Judge.** ⟶ *Verse 8*
Give us the **fullness** of   **life**   for   **ever** with all who are   **yours.** ⟶ *Antiphon II*

AFTER THE LAST ANTIPHON—TO BE SUNG BY ALL:
(○ = ○ *of verses*)

(*Choir in harmony*)   AL - LE - LU - IA,   AL - LE - LU - IA!

See also the Melody Version for Congregation, overleaf

MELODY VERSION FOR CONGREGATION

TE DEUM LAUDAMUS

(The words in italics are sung by the Choir alone)

(Antiphon I)   *Extol the Lord your God,*
for the Lord your God is holy.

VERSES 1-5

1   **You** we **praise** as **God;**
you we ac-**claim** as **Lord;**
you the **whole** earth **worships,**
e- **ternal Father** of **all.**

Extol the Lord your God, ...

2   To **you** all **orders** of **being,**
every pow'r that **is,**
those who wait **closest** upon you
raise their **endless cry:**

3   **Holy, Holy, Holy,**
Captain of the **heav'nly armies,**
all **time** and **space,** and be**yond,**
re- **flect** your **kingly glory!**

Extol the Lord your God, ...

4   The **shining dance** of your **messengers,**
your **prophets' song** of **praise,**
the **white**-robed **army** who **died** for you,
the **Church** throughout the **world,**

5   pro- **claim** their **faith** in **you,**
Father of **might** un-**bounded,**
Son, alone to be **worshipped,**
Spirit, sent to our **aid.**

(Antiphon II)   *Who is the King of Glory?*
              The Lord of Hosts, he is the King of Glory!

6   You, **Christ**, are the **King** of **Glory**,
      you are the **Father's eternal Son**.
        When to **save** the **world** you became **man**,
     you did not **shrink** from a **human birth**.

               Who is the King of Glory? . . .

7   By de- **stroying** the **sting** of **death**
    you gave be- **lievers** a **road** to God's **presence**,
    where you **sit enthroned** in **light**;
       we a- **wait** your **coming** as **Judge**.

8   **Bought** at the **price** of your **life**
      we your **household pray** for your **help**:
         Give us the **fullness** of **life**
      for **ever** with **all** who are **yours**.

       Who is the King of Glory? . . .
       The Lord of Hosts, he is the King of Glory!

ALL SING:

AL – LE – LU – IA!   AL-LE – LU – IA!

From the Latin of about A.D. 400
Tr. Alan Luff (1928-)

101 Psalm 23

('The Lord is my Shepherd')

JOSEPH GELINEAU (1920–

VERSES 1–2
Unison

1 The Lord is my Shepherd; there is nothing I shall **want**.
2 He guides me a-long the right path; he is **true** to his **name**.

Fresh and green are the pastures where he gives me re-pose.
If I should walk in the valley of darkness, no evil would I fear.

Near restful waters he leads me, to re-vive my drooping spi-rit.
You are there with your crook and your staff; with these you give me com-fort.

VERSES 3–5
Unison

3 You have pre-pared a banquet for me in the sight of my foes.
4 Surely goodness and kindness shall follow me all the days of my life.
5 To the Father and Son give glory, give glory to the Spirit.

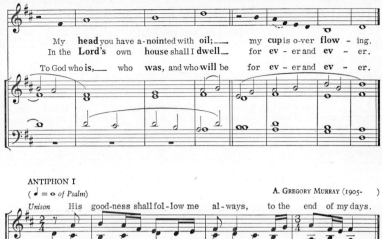

My **head** you have a-nointed with **oil;**___ my **cup** is o-ver **flow** – ing,
In the **Lord's** own house shall I **dwell**___ for ev – er and **ev** – er.
To God who **is,**___ who **was,** and who **will** be for ev – er and **ev** – er.

ANTIPHON I
(♩ = ○ *of Psalm*)

A. GREGORY MURRAY (1905-   )

Unison His good-ness shall fol-low me al-ways, to the end of my days.

ANTIPHON II
(♩ = ○ *of Psalm*)

A. GREGORY MURRAY

Unison The Lord___ is my Shep-herd, no-thing shall I want: he

leads me by safe___ paths, no-thing shall I fear.

102

Psalm 24

('The Lord's is the earth')

JOSEPH GELINEAU (1920–   )

VERSES 1–3
Unison or Harmony

Org.

1 The Lord's is the earth and its fullness, the world and
2 Who shall climb the mountain of the Lord? Who shall stand in his
3 He shall re-ceive_____ blessings from the Lord and re-ward from the

all its peoples. It is he_____ who set it on the seas;
holy place? The man with clean hands and pure heart,
God who saves him. Such are the men_____ who seek him,

Vv. 1 & 2 | V. 3

on the waters he made it firm.
who de - sires not worthless things.
seek the face of the God of ————→ Ja - cob.

VERSES 4-8
Unison or Harmony

4 O gates, lift high your heads; grow higher, ancient
5 Who is the King of Glory? The Lord, the mighty, the
6 O gates, lift high your heads; grow higher, ancient
7 Who is he, the King of Glory? He, the Lord of
8 Give glory to the Father Al - mighty, to his Son, Jesus Christ, the

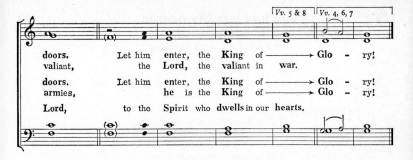

Vv. 5 & 8 ‖Vv. 4, 6, 7

doors.   Let him enter, the **King** of ⟶ **Glo** - ry!
valiant,   the **Lord,** the **valiant** in **war.**

doors.   Let him enter, the **King** of ⟶ **Glo** - ry!
armies,   he is the **King** of ⟶ **Glo** - ry!

Lord,   to the **Spirit** who **dwells** in our **hearts.**

ANTIPHON I
(♩ = 𝅝 of Psalm)   A. GREGORY MURRAY (1905-   )

Seek   the   face   of   the   Lord,   and   yearn   for   him.

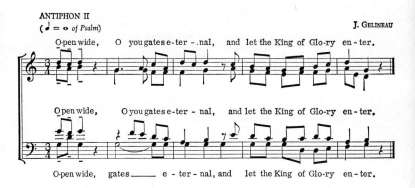

ANTIPHON II
(♩ = 𝅝 of Psalm)   J. GELINEAU

O-pen wide,   O you gates e-ter - nal,   and let the King of Glo-ry en - ter.

O-pen wide,   O you gates e-ter - nal,   and let the King of Glo-ry en - ter.

O-pen wide,   gates____ e-ter-nal, and   let the King of Glo-ry en - ter.

It is suggested that Antiphon I be sung in conjunction with verses 1-3, and Antiphon II with verses 4-8.

103 'Jesus has left his people . . .'

A Poem for Choral Speaking

'I will not leave you comfortless: I will come to you'

Congregation	Jesus has left his people; Our King will not defend us. Lord, why hast thou forsaken us, Now fears and passions rend us?
Minister *& Choir*	O remember his own word: 'The servant shall be as his Lord'. Forsaken Christ, we triumph in thee!
All	*Alleluia!*
Congregation	We never saw thee healing. We never heard thee preaching. O, could we feel thy wounded hand, Could we but ask thy teaching!
Minister *& Choir*	He himself foresaw our need. 'Unseeing faith is blest indeed'. Our Lord! Our God! we bow before thee!
All	*Alleluia!*
Congregation	Lord, we have banned ourselves from thee, Hearts closed against our neighbour. Thou art the leper, refugee, Stranger in humblest labour.
Minister *& Choir*	Rise! He's knocking at our door; He comes now as he came before. 'In broken bread I give you my life'.
All	*Alleluia!*
Congregation	Our Master has abandoned us. We cannot save the dying. Men live to self and lose their life; Must we now leave them lying?
Minister *& Choir*	Courage! Jesus comes to stay. 'Far better I should go away. Receive my Spirit. Save by my Power'.
All	*Alleluia!*

Emily Chisholm (1910-   )

104 An Offertory Canticle

('Thine, O Lord, is the greatness')

Unison. ♩=60–70.

RICHARD CHUBB (1945–)

Thine, O Lord, is the great-ness and the pow'r and the glo-ry and the vic-t'ry and the ma-je-sty. All that is in the hea-vens and the earth is thine. All things

104 (*continued*)

An Offertory Canticle
('**Thine, O Lord, is the greatness**')

come of thee, O   Lord, and of thine own have we gi - ven   thee!

Music: © *Richard Chubb*

THINE, O Lord, is the greatness and the power
  and the glory and the victory and the majesty.

All that is in the heavens and the earth is thine.

All things come of thee, O Lord,
  and of thine own have we given thee!

From I *Chronicles,*
  chapter 29, *vv.* II *and* 14.

SUPPLEMENTARY TUNES
for
Hymns in THE METHODIST HYMN BOOK

1

M.H.B. 612 Lead, kindly Light

ALBERTA 10 4.10 4.10 10.   WILLIAM H. HARRIS (1883–   )
Unison

1 Lead, kind-ly Light, a - mid th'en-circling gloom Lead thou me on! The night is dark and I am far from home; Lead thou me on! Keep thou my feet; I do not ask to see

Music: © *Oxford University Press*

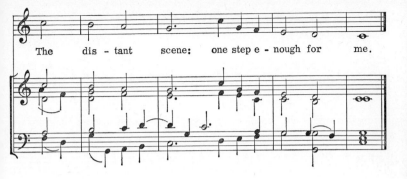

The   dis – tant   scene: one step e – nough for   me.

2   **M.H.B. 612 Lead, kindly Light**

LUX BENIGNA 10 4.10 4.10 10.   J. B. DYKES (1823–76)

3 M.H.B. 431 Love divine, all loves excelling

ARFON 87.87.D.

Traditional melody, found
both in Wales and in France.

1 Love di-vine, all loves ex-cel-ling, Joy of heav'n, to earth come down;

Fix in us thy hum-ble dwel-ling, All thy faithful mer-cies crown:

Je-su, thou art all com-pas-sion, Pure, un-bounded love thou art;

Vi-sit us with thy sal-va-tion, En-ter ev-ery trem-bling heart.

4   M.H.B. 290   **Gracious Spirit, Holy Ghost**
         297   **Come to our poor nature's night**

BONCHURCH 777.5.   W. R. PASFIELD (1909–   )

Music: © *W. R. Pasfield*

5   M.H.B. 50   **The Lord's my Shepherd, I'll not want**

CRIMOND C.M.   Melody attributed to JESSIE S. IRVINE (1836–87,
                                Harmonized by WILLIAM McKIE (1947)

6   M.H.B. 249   In the Name of Jesus

CAMBERWELL 65.65.D.   MICHAEL BRIERLEY (1932–)

HARMONY VERSION

1 In the Name of Je sus_____ Ev- ery knee shall bow, _____

UNISON VERSION (*Marziale—moderately fast*)

C   F6 G7   C   F   Em G7   C G C G

Ev- ery tongue con-fess him_ King of Glo - ry now._____

Am   Dm   Em7 C Eb7   G   D7   G   C G7

'Tis the Fa-ther's pleasure___ We should call him Lord, ___ Who from the be-

C   F6 G7   C   C7   F   E7   Am   Dm   G7 F6

Vv. 1-4   V. 5

ginning Was the migh-ty Word.___   now.___

Vv. 1-4   V. 5

C   Dm   C   G7   C   p   Dm   Em G7   C   A♭ Dm7 G7   C

7   M.H.B. 308   Lord, thy word abideth

CHESTERTON   GEOFFREY BEAUMONT (1903–)

Unison. Vv. 1, 3, 5 start here

1 Lord, thy word a - bi-deth, And our foot-steps gui-deth,

Who its truth be-liev-eth Light and joy re - ceiv - eth. 2 When our

foes are near us, Then thy word doth cheer us, Word of con-so - la - tion,

Message of sal - va - tion.   near thee!

Music: © *W. Paxton & Co. Ltd.*

8

M.H.B. 386   O Thou who camest from above

HEREFORD L.M.   S. S. WESLEY (1810–76)

1 O Thou who cam-est from a-bove The pure ce-les - tial fire_ to im-part, Kin - dle a fire_ of sac - red love On the mean al - tar of_ my heart!

M.H.B. 525   **Through the love of God our Saviour**

EAST ACKLAM   84.84.888.4.   FRANCIS JACKSON (1917–   )

1 Through the love of   God our Sa-viour, All___ will be   well;

Free and changeless is his fa-vour, All,___ all is   well:

Pre-cious is the blood that healed us; Per-fect is the grace that sealed us;

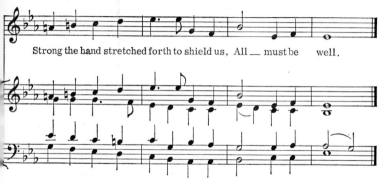

Strong the hand stretched forth to shield us, All __ must be well.

Music: © Francis Jackson

10 M.H.B. 647 **Lord, it belongs not to my care**
  485 **I'm not ashamed to own my Lord**

HARESFIELD C.M.   J. DYKES BOWER (1905–   )
Broadly

Music: © J. Dykes Bower

H

HARVEY

GEOFFREY BEAUMONT (1903–)

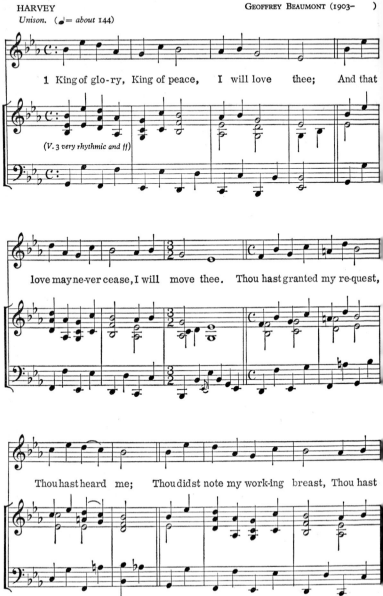

spared me.   -tol   thee.

12   M.H.B. 222   Our Lord is risen from the dead!

HEDLEY   L.M. and Alleluia   K. N. NAYLOR (1931–   )

1 Our Lord is ri - sen from the dead! Our Je - sus is__ gone

up__ on high! The pow'rs of hell are cap - tive led, Dragged

to   the por - tals of__ the sky.   *Al - le - lu – ia!*

M.H.B. 339 & 340   Come, O thou Traveller unknown

ISRAEL 88.88.88.

FRANCIS WESTBROOK (1903–   )

1 Come, O thou Tra-vel-ler un - known, Whom still I hold, but can - not see! My com-pa – ny before is gone, And I am left a - lone— with thee; With thee all night I

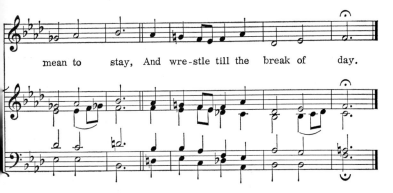

mean to   stay, And wre-stle till the   break of   day.

14   M.H.B. 794   **Eternal Son. eternal Love**
         370 { **Jesu, thy blood and righteousness**
              Jesu, be endless praise to thee

LLEDROD (LLANGOLLEN) L.M.   Traditional Welsh Hymn Melody

15

M.H.B. 701 **The Church's one foundation**
60 **Ere God had built the mountains**
979 **Our Father, by whose servants**

KING'S LYNN 76.76.D.

English Traditional Melody
Arranged by R. VAUGHAN WILLIAMS (1872–1958)

Unison

1 The Church's one foun - da - tion is Je-sus Christ her Lord;

She is his new cre - a - tion By wa-ter and the word;

From heav'n he came and sought her To be his ho-ly bride;

With his own love he bought her, And for her life he died.

Music: © Oxford University Press

16

M.H.B. 671 **Sing Alleluia forth in duteous praise**

MARTINS 10 10.7.   P. C. BUCK (1871–1947)
Unison

1 Sing Al - le - lu - ia forth in du-teous praise, O

ci - ti-zens of heav'n, and sweetly raise An end-less

Al - le - lu - ia! A - - men.

Music: © Stainer & Bell Ltd.

17

LAUS AGNO 55.55.65.65.   G. EDWARD JONES (1911–   )

1 All thanks to the Lamb,— Who gives us to meet: His

love we pro - claim, His prai - ses re - peat; We

own him our Je - sus, Con - tin - ual - ly near To

par-don and bless us, And per-fect us here. *A - men.*

Music: © G. Edward Jones

8   M.H.B. 35   **For the beauty of the earth**

LUCERNA LAUDONIAE 77.77.77.   DAVID EVANS (1874–1948)

1 For the beau - ty of the earth, For the beau - ty of the

skies, For the love which from our birth O - ver

and a - round us lies, Gra - cious God, to

thee we raise This our sac - ri - fice of praise.

19 M.H.B. 70 All my hope on God is founded

MICHAEL 87.87.337.
Unison

HERBERT HOWELLS (1892–

1 All my hope on God is founded; He doth still my trust re-new, Me through change and chance he guid-eth, On-ly good and on-ly true. God un-known, He a-

lone   Calls   my   heart   to   be___   his   own.

20   **M.H.B. 805   Christ for the world, we sing**

MILTON ABBAS   664.6664.   ERIC H. THIMAN (1900–   )

21

READING 88.88.88

FRANCIS WESTBROOK (1903–

Unison

1 Come, let us with our Lord a - rise, Our Lord, who made both earth and skies; Who died to save the world he made, And rose tri - um - phant from the dead; He

rose, the Prince of life and peace, And stamped the day for ev- er his.

Music: © *Oxford University Press*

22   M.H.B. 669   **Dear Lord and Father of mankind**

REPTON   86.88.6.
Unison

C. HUBERT H. PARRY (1848–1918)
(from a song in his oratorio *Judith*)

23

SENNEN COVE C.M.

WILLIAM H. HARRIS (1883–

Music: © *William H. Harris*

24

WARRINGTON L.M.
(Alternative to M.H.B. Version)

R. HARRISON (1748–1810)
(original harmony, except in last 2 bars)

25

M.H.B. 788 Disposer Supreme, and Judge of the earth

DISPOSER SUPREME 10 10.11 11.

J. A. SYKES (1909–62)

Moving briskly

1 Dis - po-ser Su-preme, and Judge of the earth, Who choo-sest for thine the weak and the poor; To frail earth-en ves-sels and things of no worth En-trust-ing thy ri-ches, which aye shall en-dure.

Music: © Miss C. M. Sykes

26

M.H.B. 26   Ye holy angels bright
    40   We give immortal praise
  886   To thee our God we fly

CROFT'S 136th   66.66.88.
(*Alternative to M.H.B. Version*)

Dr WILLIAM CROFT (1678–1727)
(original melody, bass and rhythm)

1 Ye ho-ly an-gels bright, Who wait at God's right hand, Or through the realms of light Fly at your Lord's com-mand, As-sist our song, Or else the theme Too high doth seem For mor-tal tongue.

INDEXES

ALPHABETICAL INDEX OF TUNES

(excluding special Song settings)

S.T. = SUPPLEMENTARY TUNES

Alphabetical Index of Tunes

METRICAL INDEX OF TUNES

(excluding special Song settings)

S.T. = SUPPLEMENTARY TUNES

S.M.

Egham, 54
Foster, 52i
Franconia, 60ii
Garelochside, 66
Hillsborough, 52ii
Redemptor, 68
St Bride, 37
St Paul's, 60i

C.M.

Bangor, 25
Chorus Angelorum, 36
Contemplation, 59
Crimond, S.T. 5
Haresfield, S.T. 10
McKee, 34
Ruth, 5
St Bernard, 18
St Botolph, 58
St Enodoc, 31
Sennen Cove, S.T. 23
This endris nyght, 19
Wesley's Chapel, 53
York, 61

L.M.

Bow Brickhill, 14
Gonfalon Royal, 69
Hereford, S.T. 8
Invitation, 51
Lansdowne, 4
Lledrod (Llangollen)
  S.T. 14
Niagara, 50
Nürnberg, 48
Penitence, 15
St Bartholomew, 47
Solemnis haec festivitas,
  57ii
Truro, 20ii

Warrington, S.T. 24
Winchester New, 57i
Woodbridge Road, 46

L.M. with Alleluias

Hedley, S.T. 12
Ilfracombe, 20i

55.55.D.

Le P'ing, 28

55.55.65.65.

Laus Agno, S.T. 17
(see also **10 10.11 11.**)

65.65.D.

Camberwell, S.T. 6
Jonathan, 85
Sutton Trinity, 74

664.6664.

Milton Abbas, S.T. 20

66.65.65.

Cambridge, 11

66.66.66.

Hail to the Lord, 30

66.66.88.

Andrew, 67i
Christchurch, 62
Croft's 136th, S.T. 26
Lawes' Psalm 47, 67ii

66.88.6.

Greestone, 6i
Requiem, 6ii

67.67.66.66.

Rinkart (Kommt Seelen),
  9

67.67.D.

Vruechten, 70

76.76.D.

King's Lynn, S.T. 15
Thornbury, 71

76.76.78.76.

Wytham, 39

777.5.

Bonchurch, S.T. 4

77.77.

Come, my Way, 12
Lauds, 64ii
Northampton, 64i
Petersfield, 35

77.77.77.

Lucerna Laudoniae,
  S.T. 18
New Horizons, 23

8.33.6.D.

Benifold, 21

84.84.888.4.

East Acklam, S.T. 9

86.88.6.

Repton, S.T. 22

87.87.

All for Jesus, 1
Birabus, 3i
Citizens, 3ii
Gott des Himmels, 45
Halton Holgate, 17ii
Lass den Brüdern, 43ii
May Hill, 43i
Ottery St Mary, 17i
Shipston, 26

Metrical Index of Tunes

INDEX OF AUTHORS, TRANSLATORS AND SOURCES OF WORDS

A number in italics indicates a Translation.

Authors, Translators and Sources of Words

INDEX OF COMPOSERS, ARRANGERS AND SOURCES OF TUNES

A number in brackets indicates a Harmonization or Arrangement.

S.T. = SUPPLEMENTARY TUNES

Composers, Arrangers and Sources of Tunes

INDEX OF SEASONS AND SUBJECTS

First Lines in the 'Songs' are in italics.

Index of Seasons and Subjects

Index of Seasons and Subjects

GENERAL INDEX

General Index

General Index

Index of Supplementary Tunes

INDEX OF SUPPLEMENTARY TUNES

HYMNS

in

THE METHODIST HYMN BOOK
which may be sung to
TUNES IN THIS BOOK